REINCARN/
IN MODERN

REINCARNATION IN MODERN LIFE

Towards a New Christian Awareness

*Six lectures given in Rome
22–25 April 1994*

Pietro Archiati

TEMPLE LODGE
London

Translated by Pauline Wehrle

Temple Lodge Publishing
51 Queen Caroline Street
London W6 9QL

Published by Temple Lodge 1997

Originally published in German under the title *Erneuertes Christentum und Wiederverkörperung* by Verlag Freies Geistesleben, Stuttgart, Germany in 1996

A catalogue record for this book is available from the British Library

ISBN 0 904693 88 0

Cover art by Rosalind Faram; cover layout by S. Gulbekian
Typeset by DP Photosetting, Aylesbury, Bucks
Printed and bound in Great Britain by Cromwell Press Limited, Broughton Gifford, Wiltshire

CONTENTS

	page
PREFACE	vii

Lecture One
BEGINNING AND END OF REPEATED LIVES
ON EARTH 1

Lecture Two
BETWEEN DEATH AND A NEW INCARNATION
Prenatal Preparation for Life on Earth 19

Lecture Three
ARE THERE INDICATIONS OF REINCARNATION
IN THE GOSPELS?
The Christ-Event and repeated Earth Lives 40

Lecture Four
METAMORPHOSES OF LOVE AND HATE IN
THREE SUCCESSIVE LIVES 56

Lecture Five
DAILY LIFE, SOCIAL RELATIONSHIPS AND
REINCARNATION 77

Lecture Six
REINCARNATION, CHRIST'S RESURRECTION
AND THE RESURRECTION OF THE BODY 98

NOTES 123

PREFACE

These lectures were part of a conference taking place in Rome in the spring of 1994, to an audience of about five hundred people from all over Italy. Each lecture was followed by a lengthy, often lively conversation.

I am attempting to show, in a form everyone can understand, that an awareness of reincarnation and karma is essential if Christianity is to be alive in the present and the future.

Even everyday practical life and our social contacts become at one and the same time decidedly more 'Christian' and more 'human' if we have not only a theoretical knowledge of reincarnation and karma but our heart forces live with it.

The reader should just imagine what happens if one's thoughts are recast from one language to another *twice*: from German to Italian and back again. One is almost forced, repeatedly, to rise from the language-bound level of word formations and idiomatic expressions to the universal level of thoughts. Now that these lectures are to be published I have gone to the trouble of revising them thoroughly.

In the course of the conference I proposed a symposium in which representatives of Buddhism, natural science, Catholicism and anthroposophy all gave their views on reincarnation. The representative of the Catholic Church did not have anything to say *against* reincarnation and expressed an extreme relativism: there are many thought forms and everybody has his own; reincarnation is also one among many.

The following day many of the participants were indignant with disappointment and, in order to pacify them, I found I had to discuss the semi-official position of the Catholic Church. The mood in the hall felt a bit belligerent. The reader will sense this in my words — especially in the last lecture.

Pietro Archiati
Unterlengenhardt, 1 February 1996

Lecture One

BEGINNING AND END OF REPEATED LIVES ON EARTH

The theme we shall be talking about today is not a simple one; for I want to bring, in an informative way to begin with, what Rudolf Steiner's spiritual science tells us of the beginning and end of repeated lives on earth.

I should like to begin with a few general thoughts which have to do with a change in our consciousness, with a new level of consciousness in humanity—thoughts aimed at helping us understand why the question of reincarnation has become so topical recently (and to all appearances will become even more so in the future), why people are talking about and discussing it at all. And furthermore why, a hundred or two hundred years ago, this question was almost non-existent on a cultural level in the West.

I shall therefore present what I have to say in two parts. In the first part we shall think about this new phenomenon which has come among humanity, this inclination to talk about reincarnation. In the second part, which will be a bit more complex, I will try, at least in broad outline, to point to the factors of evolution which have brought about the beginning of what we call earth life and those which will lead to their end.

I shall start with the new threshold of consciousness which western humanity has reached and out of which we ask: does a human being really incarnate only once? This house of clay—if we want to call it that—this house which we call 'the human body', do we build it just a single time or several times? We know for certain that we do it *once*. We only need to pinch ourselves to realize we have a body. By doing this each one of us can experience right now that we are incarnated. What we are asking is whether there have been other times when we have done what we have obviously done this time. Is it founded on the logic of evolution that we human beings undertake incarnation just one single time or is the reverse the case, and we are actually bound to go through incarnation several times?

A third possibility would of course also be conceivable, namely, an endless repetition of earth lives *ad infinitum*. We should also consider this.

Looked at from the standpoint of an evolving con-sciousness, why is the question of reincarnation of such importance both from a cultural and a sociological point of view? I should like to draw your attention to two significant factors in the make-up of a modern person: firstly his inner attitude to his past, and secondly the way he faces what is going to happen to him in the future.

Let us take a look at the attitude people of today have to their past, to what they have become as a result of what they have made of what life has offered them, and then let us look at the way present-day people normally envisage their future.

When we consider these two dimensions of our existence we notice — and in this shape and form this is something quite new! — that nowadays people are becoming less and less capable of accepting the unpleasant sides either of themselves just as they are or of the things round about them. There is an increasing rejection of and rebellion against destiny. People show a certain intolerance, a kind of rebelliousness, if things are not just to their liking, an unwillingness to approve of the way things are. We know that in earlier centuries people found it easier to accept their destiny. They possessed the ability to resign themselves to fate — whether this should be assessed positively or nega-tively is not the issue here. We do not wish to make moral evaluations, but merely to state the fact that at a certain stage of evolution this was so. This ability is being rapidly lost today.

In the past everything was put down to Providence, or to God's unfathomable command and will, or destiny. All these ideas which helped people reconcile themselves to the inevitabilities of existence have been increasingly losing their hold over people in recent years. In the past a person not only accepted and put up with himself as he was, but also his neighbours and his life circumstances. In recent times, however, everything points to the fact that, quite generally, insurgence and intolerance are on the increase everywhere. People are increasingly becoming less and less willing to accept things as they are. If someone is born poor and is forced from an economic point of view to lead a more modest life than someone else, he is annoyed and asks: why should he have everything while I have nothing? Why this 'injustice'? We must ask ourselves to what extent this rebellion leads to a solution of the problem and in how far this attitude is right and human in the light of the objective fact that the one person is enormously rich and the other is destitute. We shall see how important it is to acquire a certain inner calm, for a state of emotion is the very thing that hinders us from seeing things objectively.

Where the future (i.e. that which is still undetermined) is concerned, we can see in the people of today a further basic attitude which in a sense is even more alarming. I mean the inability to imagine that the effects of one's actions will at some time fall back on oneself. A certain irresponsibility and thoughtlessness are on the increase in humanity, a certain recklessness in everyday life which appears to come from the fact that people think that life marches on with a kind of determinism irrespective of their actions.

To take an extreme example: if one person kills another, and in a brutal way as well—and there are endless examples of this in the world right now—in the majority of cases he does this without it ever occurring to him whether in further course the consequences of this action of his could ever come back to him.

In earlier times there were moral impediments, commandments or respected traditions whose functions were to keep a person from doing certain deeds. Nowadays a person can commit actions which he could not have done so easily 40, 20 or even 10 years ago. I think this change in our attitude of mind is of the greatest significance, for it brings with it a fundamental change in the way we human beings relate to one another. Life is quite different in a society where everyone is afraid of doing inhuman acts of violence than it is in a society where there is no longer this fear and people are prepared to do anything, the only authority able to prevent a person from committing certain actions being a law-imposed punishment—though even this is no longer based on a law which comes from the divine or spiritual world but one that is negotiated on a human level and which, just because it is made by human beings, is constantly open to question.

Present-day people know very little about the possible consequences of their actions. They only think of the immediate ones because these are directly obvious. They know nothing about forces which may perhaps show their effects much later on, for example the law stipulating that the constellation of moral forces out of which one person kills another comes into effect again after possibly several centuries, by which time, although he is the same person, his whole nature will have undergone a complete change.

We can characterize the present level of human consciousness with two forcible, only too familiar concepts: 'egoism' and 'materialism'. Egoism here is in the sense of the widespread belief that other people's loss is my gain. The main characteristic of egoism is of course that you are convinced that your own advantage is acquired at the expense of others. The important thing to ask with regard to egoism is whether this is actually true or are we under an illusion. If I can gain an advantage because someone else is at a disadvantage, why should I renounce my advantage? Who says I should? A moral law? Who brought this into force? I shall certainly not try to overcome egoism unless I am convinced that egoism is an illusion and that this illusion consists in believing that it will not be me who is the first to lose out if I try to acquire things at the expense of others. We have to find a reason showing why it will only be myself who loses out.

The following question immediately comes to mind. Is it not the case that people who try to reap an advantage for themselves at the expense of others are often very successful in life? This is true of course if we look at the span of a single life. It does not appear to be an illusion; it seems to work.

Materialism is the second characteristic feature of the present stage of human evolution. We are right in the middle of evolution—and the fundamental character of the present evolutionary stage is that humanity has sunk further into matter than ever before. The fact that human beings have never been so dependent on the material world as they are today, that they have never before identified themselves so totally with the world of matter, is what we call materialism.

What is the significance, the consequence, of human beings coming to the point of thinking that matter is the only reality and spirit is only semblance? This view means that a person who considers himself intelligent will assume that the chief aim in life is to grab as much as he can and get as much pleasure out of it as possible. Possessions and power become the goal of life. Examples of this are plain to see today. Without any intention of condemning or moralizing, we just want to state as a fact that the mentality of accumulating and enjoying as also of acquiring power is very widespread. In the face of this fact it is useless to point a finger of scorn at people and say: No, you may not do that, it is not moral. We shall in fact realize that it is good such a thing does not achieve anything any more, for commands coming from outside were justified only in humanity's stage of childhood. When a human being comes of age, however, he needs to be sure that if he resolves to act in a certain way he will be contributing to his own good and working at the improvement of his own being. Therefore the only morally good reason for doing or leaving something is the human being himself.

The only certain basis for an action which does not arise out of moralizing is the endeavour to reach the wholeness of our being by assuming that each one of us aspires to this by nature. For if we were to imagine there were a kind of person who aimed to be less rather than more, we should be beyond all rationality; I should be at a loss for words. As long as we can assume it to be true that everybody aspires to get closer and closer to the wholeness of their being, then all that there remains for us to do is to persevere with asking about and fathoming this wholeness of human nature. It is then up to each individual to make the effort to strive for it.

Goodness, every act of moral goodness, is what makes a person more human. This is why it is good. For man himself is the sum of all moral goodness. There is no moral goodness outside man for human beings cannot be more than human. In the human world there can be nothing greater or better than human beings. Therefore that which is morally bad is everything which makes us less human, everything which drags our being down.

The path of knowledge which leads to the discovery of what enables a human being to achieve the wholeness of his being, what adds to and what diminishes from his being, is not an easy path; yet it is the only one that grants us an understanding, without moralizing, of what each individual really wants and what he does not want.

If we reckon with reincarnation, today's change in

consciousness consists of the following. Let us assume for the moment that human beings incarnate more than once. Just now we will consider it as a hypothesis. If it is true that I am not here on earth for the first time, but that my life, consisting of everything I have myself become, the way in which I have arranged my life, the circumstances and the people I live among, all this is by and large a *result* of my previous lives, then the whole manner of my relation to my past would utterly change. Instead of being impatient and rebelling against so many things which I do not like, which do not appeal to me as they are, there would arise in me, by degrees, a totally different outlook, enabling me to realize that I myself have wanted all this to be as it is. All that I am, everything that happens to me, everything that surrounds me, is as I wanted. I myself am the cause of everything I encounter, for if it had nothing to do with me, if it were not attracted to my being, it would pass me by without my noticing it.

With regard to the future also, a completely different attitude would arise. I would have the conviction that all my actions will come back to me some time or another. I cannot have a single thought, feeling or will impulse, or perform a single action, without the corresponding real, spiritual consequences rebounding on me, i.e. without a real change coming about in my being, because by means of my thoughts, feelings, will impulses and actions I am constantly changing my whole constitution as far as the forces at work in me are concerned. This means, however, that with my changed being I attract other life situations, other human relationships, other encounters. For example, if I cheat another person, I shall have to do with him again in my next life, until I have learnt that I cannot have privileges that are to the detriment of others.

Looked at from this perspective one lifetime is like a day. So, to acquire an awareness of the fact of reincarnation is similar to extending our consciousness whereby we look at the totality of one earth life in the way we usually look at a day. Between one day and another there is also always a break in consciousness. When we are asleep we are not conscious. When we wake up in the morning we take possession of our body again; we do not build it up once more from scratch — we simply make use of it again.

How does today proceed compared to yesterday? There has been a break, of course, yet we know there is absolute continuity, for today I still have the skills that I had yesterday and I meet with the same life situation I was in yesterday; yesterday's problems face me afresh today.

And yet something has changed, for today the results of my actions yesterday face me in the form of causes. For instance, yesterday I made the final arrangement for the furnishing of this room and today the room is ready. It has not disappeared! There is such a thing as a chain of events in which consequences become causes and causes lead to consequences.

Could it be that by extending our consciousness we discover that there is a series of earth lives which are linked together in a similar connection of cause and effect as the single days of a lifetime, so that what previously appeared to be so irrational appears now to be all of a sudden not so irrational after all?

If this were the case we should have an answer for all those people who give a resigned sigh and say: Oh! There is no justice in this world! A crook makes a good life for himself, he succeeds all round. But just look at the other fellow; he has always done good, and yet he is plagued by one illness after another. Is that just? If we are honest we have to admit that there is really no 'justice' in life, in *one* life.

If we consider the phenomena with the composure of a person who is endeavouring to reach the objective facts, we must confess that looking at it from the vantage point of an ordinary human being within one lifetime there is actually the utmost *injustice*. But this also applies in a row of successive days. In the course of a single day we cannot sort everything out satisfactorily either. On this small scale too we cannot always round off everything in one single day.

Looking at the matter on a large scale we can say similarly: Not everything is rounded off in one lifetime!

It is not a question of proving reincarnation. If it is a fact then it can be just as little 'proved' as any other reality. The existence of trees is also a fact and yet nobody has as yet proved that there are trees, for one *cannot* prove that trees exist. Nor can we 'prove' logically how the single days in the course of a life are related. There is nothing there to prove. If someone is in the position to have the experience of how those particular days relate to one another, then he knows from experience and can talk about it — but he can prove nothing.

What we have to do is to extend our view of life to such a degree that we are capable of seeing and experiencing life as a unit in the same way as we usually envisage and experience a day as a unit. Just as we relate one day to another, to the previous or the following one — we all have plenty of experience at this level of consciousness — let us ask ourselves: What would transpire if we were to consider the sum total of a life in the way we are in the habit of looking at the sum total of a day, and how would this long day relate to the one preceding it and following it?

Psychology has known for a long time that the period of time passing between cause and effect can be very long. Nevertheless it is always relatively short, of course, for it does not extend beyond the boundaries of one lifetime.

For how long have psychologists been going back 50 years in search of the causes of symptoms which appear in 50-year-olds! The thought is no longer new that it is a mistake to look for the causal occurrence in the immediately preceding occurrences, and that this view is justified at most with mechanical procedures.

In the realm of mechanics and material things the cause always immediately precedes the effect. If I have two balls and I roll one towards the other, stationary one, then the action causing the effect is the push. Cause and effect must in a certain way coincide. On the human level, however, I can prepare the ground for something the effect of which I want to happen only in 15 years time. In the human kingdom we do not have this instantaneous effect such as we have in mechanics, for example in the case of a push. That is why psychologists say: To understand this phenomenon in the behaviour of the 50-year-old I have to investigate a long way back; I have to look for the causes of the present behaviour when this person was five or three or two years of age.

This is just one example to show that in recent times people have realized that they have to extend over a longer time span their research regarding the connection between cause and effect. I consider this path psychologists have adopted to be the beginning of a far-reaching and far more comprehensive study of the connection between cause and effect!

If we begin to think that within the span of a lifetime only the small things can be explained, namely, those which arise from today to tomorrow, but not the whole of my existence as it is today, and if the thought were to arise that maybe, centuries ago, during another long day which I spent on earth and which we call a 'life', I set the scene for everything that I have in the way of health, bodily characteristics, nationality, the family I belong to and the things which happen to me — if we start thinking in this way — then we begin in our thoughts to step beyond the 'boundaries' of birth and death.

Birth and death are the two boundaries we come to when we start to leave behind us the narrow-mindedness that restricts our search for cause and effect to one lifetime. Then we immediately come to such questions as: Why was I born with black skin, or white? Why was I born rich? Why poor? Why were both my parents alcoholics? Why was I born Russian, or American? Why?

You all know the answer that was traditionally given by religion if a person raised the question of 'why' with regard to the things that determined the situation into which he was born and which he was stuck with for life. The answer was: Because God created you that way. And if he was told further that God's decree is unfathomable, this is an answer that satisfies modern mankind less and less. More and more people are saying: God Himself must have definite and very good reasons why He treats one person so differently from another. He must have just and valid reasons why He allows one person and not another to be born into a situation that promises him a good chance of developing his abilities; if He equips one person with abilities and talents from the start, and not the other.

This is just an indication of the questions arising when one considers the situation a person is born into, the given circumstances belonging to his birth. Let us now look at the other gate, the one through which a human being departs from life.

Just think of what awaits a person such as 'Judas' when he dies. Does he go to hell? Does he still have the chance to progress? If he can continue to develop, how does this actually proceed? If a further development in actual human terms, that is, in real freedom, is possible for a Judas, can this happen even if he does not incarnate again? In that case why did he incarnate that time? If Judas could partake of further human development similar to ours in every respect while in a body-free condition, that is, without experiencing directly everything we can only experience in a state of incarnation, why did human beings enter into material existence at all?

I am sure you all know that more and more people—

many Catholics for instance—have great difficulty accepting the thoughts of eternal damnation. This leads to a question closely connected with reincarnation: When a very wicked person dies does he really have no opportunity any more to be redeemed, or rather, of making further progress?

At the present stage of evolution each one of us when we die is actually right at the beginning of his or her evolution. Each of us nowadays dies very unfinished. Indeed, if a person knows himself in a true and objective way, he will notice in himself an endless number of possibilities and aptitudes he would like to develop further. Perhaps he wants to be a paragon of love, or a learned man, or a great artist. He has to admit that at the time of his death he is still at the very beginning, because he has only been able to develop a minute fraction of the potential dormant within him. And what about all the rest?

If we look at the matter from the point of view of good and evil we are bound to say—and again we exclude all moralizing—that nowadays everyone, even a saint, has in him when he dies a great deal that is good and a great deal that is bad, because evolution is a long way from being finished and therefore a human being's innermost core cannot yet be totally good or totally bad. Today we are in an intermediate stage of evolution in which each individual combines an endless amount of both good and bad qualities. For believers, the thought that we live only once and that at death we are consigned forever, in a completely miraculous but actually irrational way and with our full load of imperfections, to a finality of good or evil, a paradise or the damnation of hell, is a thought they find unbearable. Yet in this instance, where it is of the utmost importance to specify exactly how this functions, conceptions become extremely vague.

A Christianity that includes the fact of repeated earth lives can take its start from Christ Jesus' statement that the earth is His body.

Rudolf Steiner's spiritual science understands this statement not as a symbol but in a literally real sense. Christ turns to the earth and the elements represented by the bread and the wine, and says: 'This is my body, this is my blood.' These words are on a par with our saying with regard to the bit of material we inhabit: 'This is my body.' If someone comes along with a needle and pricks me, I say: 'That hurts me! This is me!' What do I mean by this? Am I using a metaphor? I am maintaining — in an absolutely real sense — that these hands, this larynx and so on, move in the way they do because I, as spirit, inhabit this substance and fill it with my being. In other words, what I want to say is: 'This is no corpse but my body.'

Up till now people have treated the earth as a corpse and not as though it were the body of a spiritual being. Not having as yet reached this level of consciousness they will, in traditional Christianity, hardly have heard the voice of Christ saying to us every time we do something to the earth, 'Be careful, this is my body!' — just as I say to someone about to do something to the substance of my body: 'Just a minute, this is me!'

If we take seriously the fact that the earth is the body of Christ, then we can link up with the thought of reincarnation. To live only once and then to leave the earth for ever would be disloyal to the Christ Being, for the earth is His body. The resolve to come back to the earth again and again, however, would, by comparison, be the more Christian one because it would mean our never wanting to go through evolution far away from the Christ.

Basically what Steiner says about the Christianity of the past is that it corresponded to a particular stage of the evolution of human consciousness. When our consciousness will have attained other dimensions, however, the interpretation of the Christian mystery will also be different.

We can go so far as to say, paradoxically, that the Christ has reached an infinitely higher stage of development than we have because He no longer needs to *excarnate*. The power of His love is so perfect that He can transform the corporality of the cosmos and the earth without coming to any harm—without needing to leave them again and again.

On the other hand we human beings, because we are less highly developed, come to such harm through entering into and associating with matter that we have to withdraw again and again in order to restore the balance. If the power of our love were as great as Christ's we should not need to leave the earth and nature, because in essence the earth and all its creatures, the plants and the animals are all reaching up to man. The wish of all creation is to follow the human path because it is through man that all the non-human kingdoms will rise to the human stage—for it is the human stage that is the evolutionary stage of the earth. The real evolution of humankind in freedom consists in 'humanizing' all the beings on *earth*. Thus these non-human kingdoms have allowed themselves to be bewitched in the form of the sense world, to give humankind the possibility to develop. They are waiting for human beings to repay this sacrifice by transforming the whole reality of the earth and nature and humanizing it by taking it up into their own being. You could say, in other words, that human beings will become all the more capable of loyalty to the *earth*, to the body of Christ, the stronger and more perfect they become in their spiritual being in the course of time. It is therefore not true to say that at the end of all their earthly lives human beings will no longer have anything to do with matter. On the contrary, the end of our many incarnations on earth will consist in the fact that we shall no longer lay aside our 'body' and the body of the earth, because these will have been fully spiritualized. And when human beings reach this time, when they begin no longer to lay aside their cosmic bodily sheaths because they have fully spiritualized them, they will come closer and closer to an experience of the essential nature of the resurrection.

The Resurrection Body of Christ is a sheath of such spirituality that the Christ Spirit no longer needs to lay it aside. The Resurrection Body of the Christ is a perfect image of the spirit; it is the instrument with whose help the spirit can come to expression without encountering the least resistance.

This train of thought brings us to the second basic question which I intimated. How did the course of incarnations begin? Incarnation and excarnation are actually states of consciousness in the sense that we experience birth and death as big changes in consciousness. If we were not to perceive these two gates, the gate of birth and the gate of death, as two great thresholds we should not speak of incarnation. We speak of 'incarnation' because we want to say that through birth, as also through death, there is a decisive change of consciousness. If birth and death entailed slighter transitions of consciousness we would not speak of incarnation.

The first time the human spirit combined with matter was in the period called in Rudolf Steiner's spiritual science the 'Lemurian epoch'. After the Lemurian came the 'Atlantean epoch'. What was it that existed before this point of time of which we say that it marked the beginning of incorporation into matter, the start of incarnations? Why is it said that there were no incarnations before then? Because the relation between the human spirit and matter was quite different. When human beings had lived purely spiritually for a certain time, and wanted to connect with matter again, they formed this matter themselves after their own image. They did not experience an actual 'birth'. It was as if an artist were to take a block of marble, transform it and create a work of art out of it. That is to say, before what we actually call 'incarnations', whenever human beings underwent a connection with matter it did not cause a marked change (i.e. a decided darkening of consciousness). In course of time matter became for human beings more and more impenetrable. They began experiencing the entry into matter as a sudden dimming of consciousness. This combination of the entry into matter with an intense darkening of consciousness was what they called 'birth'. Before this time this experience of 'birth' was not there. Incarnation means the increasingly intense change that occurs in consciousness when human beings, having had a purely spiritual existence, enter into connection with matter. The crucial point is a change in consciousness which occurs all of a sudden as it were at the moment the spirit begins experiencing itself and being active within the reality of matter.

When the time will come that spirit and matter begin to become more 'alike' again, then the beginning and end of the alternation with matter will be experienced more like a going to sleep and waking up and human beings will not talk of incarnation and excarnation — of birth and death — any longer in the same sense as today. In other words, we are nowadays in an intermediate stage of evolution in which spirit and matter have pulled apart and become as dissimilar and opposite as they can possibly be. We live at the time when the contrast between spirit and matter has reached its greatest point, and this is why we speak of incarnation and excarnation. We experience a very strong leap in consciousness at birth when the spirit enters matter and no less a one at death when the spirit lays matter aside.

On our entry into matter we forget everything we experienced before we came down — so much that most present-day people are of the opinion that a human being comes into existence for the first time at conception.

Shortly before the coming of Christ, Plato was convinced that to know means to remember one's experiences before birth. Plato possessed a last lingering awareness of a continuity between the existence before and after birth which was lost later on.

According to the Christian view, as it has been up till now, a human being comes into existence at the same time as his body. While there is no body there is no human being. The moment the basis is laid for the body, at conception, God creates the soul. This thought did not originate in Christianity. It is an Aristotelian thought. Aristotle – and this is why there is such a vast difference, as far as the evolution of human consciousness is concerned, between Plato and Aristotle – was the first great thinker for whom a person's bodily nature, matter, assumed such importance with regard to self-awareness that, as a good Greek, he could not imagine a human being without a material body. Therefore for Aristotle a human being was created simultaneously with his body. And how then does he live after death, when his body is no longer there? He lives on thanks to looking back in memory on his earthly experiences and his discarded body. If it were not for these memories of their experiences while in matter, human beings would, as far as their consciousness is concerned, disappear into nothingness after death.

In the Greek cultural epoch human beings felt quite at home in the physical body. This is why it was in this epoch that Christ Himself became man on the physical plane, to come to the aid of human beings in the realm where their consciousness was at home – immersed in matter. A Greek could not imagine living without a body. Therefore after death he experienced himself as being in a realm of shades, in a lowered state of consciousness and not existing as a full human being. Life after death became the equivalent of shadow existence, for it was only with the help of his body that a human being could experience himself fully.

This way of looking at things was taken up by Christianity, and for centuries people of the West believed that the thought of there being no human existence independent of matter was an integral part of Christianity. The other question, which is also a legacy of Aristotelianism, has likewise become more and more acute: If human beings are virtually indebted to matter for everything, what is left of them when they lay the body aside at death?

Perhaps we may add in this connection that regarding the dogma of the Catholic Church as such there has not up till now been a statement with reference to reincarnation. There is no dogma declaring reincarnation to be a mistake and heretical. As far as Catholic dogma is concerned the question of reincarnation is still open today.

In traditional Christianity it has always been the general conviction of course that a human being lives only once. But a general conviction is not the same as a dogma. We cannot say of a Catholic who has become convinced of reincarnation that he is violating a dogma and is a 'heretic'. Yet I myself have had ample proof that he would be regarded and treated as such by many people in the Catholic Church.

Lecture Two

BETWEEN DEATH AND A NEW INCARNATION
Prenatal Preparation for Life on Earth

One of the thoughts we followed up yesterday was this. If human beings have reached a threshold in their evolution, where they are beginning consciously to look into the question of reincarnation, this signifies an expansion and deepening of consciousness itself. People are beginning to regard life in its totality, that is, including the Whence and Whither, as a day, as one whole unit.

Even with the level of consciousness we have had up till now we regard, as mentioned before, one day as being one of a series of days. We do not say that a day is a totally incomprehensible riddle. No, we are aware of there being a Before and an After, and we see it in a systematic context which we can grasp in thought. We are used to thinking that a great many, in a way all the events of today are explainable out of what happened on the previous days, and we take it just as much for granted that everything we do today will have its definite consequences in the coming days. We are familiar with looking at a single day in this light; we are used to it.

The chief thought yesterday evening was that western humanity has arrived at a threshold where human life as a whole and the question of where we come from, how and why, are no longer looked at as unfathomable mysteries.

Along with this come the questions we have already mentioned, such as: Who designed my life in this way and not another? Why am I like I am? Why do I enjoy good health, or not? Why was I born into this particular family and not another? Why must I share my life with these particular people and not others?

People are now starting to want to get behind the sort of question which up till now was either simply accepted or regarded as God's unfathomable decree. Even if it is not everybody who is doing so, the number of people who are beginning to ask about such things is increasing all the time.

If reincarnation exists at all then it is a fact. What we are talking about here is our human *awareness* of it. We wonder in what way or whether at all human beings in other periods of history were aware of reincarnation.

In Rudolf Steiner's spiritual science reincarnation is no hypothesis but absolute reality. If we are dealing with it here as a 'hypothesis' this is solely in the nature of our approach. To anyone who is coming to grips with the thought for the first time we would say: Regard reincarnation as a working hypothesis and see what happens! Become aware of the consequences for everyday life when you assume a human being lives more than once. There will be other people for whom reincarnation is already a reality that they no longer question. Each one must establish where he stands.

We do not need to be afraid that as our knowledge and awareness increase the mystery will 'disappear'. Quite to the contrary. The more we extend our consciousness the more mysteries we shall meet! A restricted consciousness encounters fewer mysteries, but for a wider one the mysteries are endless. In the universe we live in there is never a lack of mysteries. Scepticism in this domain is basically a fear of the living consequences and not the worry that we might lose our respect for the mysteries we do not understand.

The endeavour to regard the whole of 'life's day' as one unit in a series, because one wants to discover the hidden causes behind the realities and ask precise questions regarding the future consequences of one's actions, is a sign of the developing human consciousness wanting to take over responsibility for the whole of existence.

This effort of consciousness corresponds to an inner moral strength of the ego. The Christ forces in human beings are forces of love and moral responsibility. All attempts to throw off responsibility and to make others responsible for what one has oneself caused to happen are unchristian.

A person does himself a great injustice in his attempts to excuse himself when he invents 'chance'. Anyone who speaks of chance is actually saying he does not know why something happens. But he is not justified in saying there is no explanation just because *he* cannot discover one. In this light 'chance' events are actually holes in people's thinking!

Once I know that my whole life is like a day which runs in the way I have set going, in the same way as one day proceeds directly according to the course of the preceding days of my life which, whatever they were like, I shaped myself — if I run my mind over this, I stop talking of chance, because if I did so I would mean myself! I therefore take on the responsibility for all that I have become.

Looking at the perspective of reincarnation I say to myself: I owe all that I am, not to chance but to myself. And if I had developed differently in the past the conditions for my existence today would also be quite different. In other words, every time I shift the blame for something that concerns me onto someone or something else, I have not yet found the true being of my ego, for the reality of the ego consists of the ability to take on responsibility for everything for which I am indeed responsible because I was the cause of it.

People who make other factors responsible for what they bring about live objectively in illusion. Must they overcome this? Is it solely a matter of moral duty, an external commandment to overcome illusion? No. For evolution is aimed to proceed in such a way that the consequences that follow for a person who continues living in illusion become more and more pressing until he grasps that it is in his own interests to see through the illusion and overcome it.

Therefore it is necessary we understand that as far as egoism is concerned extortionary morals have always governed humanity. In a certain way this 'extortion' is understandable. It was essential as long as human beings lacked the ability to grasp with their reason that it does not pay to be one-sidedly egoistic. Once a person has grasped this rationally then entirely out of himself he will no longer want to be egoistic in a negative sense. He no longer needs to be told: You should not be egoistic! He will in fact not *want* to be selfish any more! The only way of overcoming egoism properly in its negative form is to realize that egoism does not pay and therefore cannot be wanted by a person's true ego.

In the parable of the prodigal son the only reason why the son decides to return is a thoroughly 'egoistic' one. In fact Christ gives us just one single reason, and it is an egoistic one. The prodigal son realizes that things could not be any worse, that even his father's hired servants fare better than he, and that is why he returns. That, however, is the most moral reason of all, for the greatest moral good is the wholeness of a person's being. There is nothing else that is truly morally good. Each one of us is called upon to attain the wholeness of his being. And if the overcoming of a particular form of egoism is part of this, then you overcome it—not in order to stop living for yourself, but because it is necessary in order to reach the wholeness of your being. The principle of both pure Christianity and pure humanity is to love your neighbour as yourself.

This is the first Christian aspect that arises when you become aware of reincarnation. A person who is conscious of reincarnation becomes more human because he takes on the moral responsibility that will bring his ego to a much greater wholeness.

Becoming conscious of the fact of reincarnation and of life in accordance with reincarnation makes a person at one and the same time more 'human' and more Christian. The decision to sheathe oneself over and over again in a physical body is at the same time the decision to remain loyal to the earth and to Christ who has made the earth His body.

It is with reference to this that Rudolf Steiner distinguishes, as he says, between 'religions of redemption' and 'resurrection religions'. What he means by this is that pre-Christian religions were pre-eminently religions of redemption in the sense that according to their original teaching the highest human ideal and goal one could aspire to was to strip off all earthly attachments, leave the world of matter, foster no more sensual desires, harbour no further wish for earthly existence, have no further use for all this and to live in consequence in a purely spiritual world, where there is no question of redeeming and transforming *the earth itself*. In other words, in the original form of Buddhism, for instance, the human being awaits a salvation that is not concerned with the fate of the earth. The destiny of the earth and the realms of nature are not important in pre-Christian religions.

The Christian religion, on the other hand, is a 'resurrection religion' just because the transformation of the earth is a *central* part of it. The ultimate goal of Christianity, the aim of human evolution, is the transformation of the earth, its gradual spiritualization. Therefore in the Christian view human evolution is not possible without interaction with the bodily sheaths and all the beings of nature.

Christ's meaning of Christian is the love of the spirit for matter, the reciprocal interpenetration of spirit and matter. That is Christian. What is pre-Christian is the spirit's 'fear' of the abysmal depths of matter, the damnation of matter as 'evil' and the longing to be 'released' from it. As distinct from this, the greatest ego force can be seen in the fact that the ego is not only no longer afraid of matter but loves it and knows that its true evolution consists in a redeeming love for the stones, the plants and the animals.

Therefore to reincarnate is actually to say 'yes' to the force of one's true ego, which is no longer afraid of the material world but loves it because it is the only place where the human spirit can *become* more and more human. So reincarnation is the basic prerequisite for loyalty to Christ, who has made the earth his body for ever, and loyalty to nature and the earth as a condition of mankind's loyalty to themselves. This opens up totally new perspectives, for ecology also.

In the eastern pre-Christian conception of rebirth people had not yet reached the full experience of the ego. If we look at Buddhism in its original form, that is, at what Buddha said to humanity in the sixth century BC, we shall recognize that the ego is described as the greatest of illusions (Rudolf Steiner speaks about this in his cycle of lectures *From Jesus to Christ*,* Karlsruhe, 1911). I myself, when I lived in the East, had many conversations with Buddhist monks, and the most contentious matter was always that of the ego. At this point we simply had to admit that our opinions differed. The most important thing for Christian civilization is the human individuality, and from their angle this is basically depicted as the greatest illusion.

In Buddhism we find the law of *transmigration of souls* (metempsychosis), that is, the soul passing in the course of evolution from one body to another, whereas by *reincarnation* is meant the evolutionary law of the human *spirit*—the I—as an individual being. The people of those days found it so difficult to accept the repeated return of the human soul

---

* Rudolf Steiner Press, London 1991.

into the world of matter—as distinct from the Christian perspective—that they envisaged salvation in the extinguishing of the thirst for existence and in the speediest possible end of the series of rebirths.

These are just the barest indications of the differences existing between the eastern and the Christian conception of reincarnation. With Steiner reincarnation assumes characteristic features that are only possible within Christianity. We need only mention two fundamental differences: on the one side a limited number of earth lives and the doctrine of the ego as the essential being of man and the goal of evolution, and on the other hand an eternal repetition of rebirths and the doctrine of the ego as the greatest illusion.

We now turn to the following question: What awaits a human being when he dies? What happens to him in the interval of time between death and a new birth?

Let us go back to the comparison with a single day. There we saw that after each day has run its course we have a break in consciousness, a transition from one kind of existence to another, and that in the morning when we wake up we pick things up again where we left off the previous evening. In a certain sense there is a new start, but there is no doubt about there being an underlying connection between what happened yesterday and what happens today.

According to Rudolf Steiner the interval between death and a new birth normally runs into centuries; the length of time a human being spends in an excarnated condition, i.e. body-free, is thus considerably longer, usually, than the time spent in incarnation, in a body-bound existence. The sun enters a new sign of the zodiac every 2160 years. The evolutionary conditions on the earth are in consequence fundamentally different after every 2160 years.

Every human being has the chance of incarnating in each of these different periods. Human beings must not skip one, because each one of them is governed by different evolutionary conditions, all of which are essential to their growth as human beings and the perfecting of their ego being. It would be unthinkable, for example, that a human individuality should not be given the opportunity to incarnate at a time in which technology and science are making the kind of progress they are today. For by living in this world of science and technology, in the world of computers and machines, human beings acquire evolutionary possibilities they would not otherwise have. I am not saying that everything we have to 'thank' science and technology for can be assessed as positive. What I mean is that through being involved with science and technology human beings have the possibility of making certain quite definite strides in their development which they could not make without this world of machines. They can also miss out on these steps, however, because they live in freedom.

Within the span of 2160 years each human being incarnates twice as a rule, once as a woman and once as a man — though obviously, as with everything that is living and not theoretical, there are numerous exceptions. People sometimes ask why the world population is constantly increasing. There is no increase in the total number of human beings. This number has always remained constant ever since there have been individual egos. We must of course add the two groups together. On the one hand there are the human beings in incarnation, the people who have bodies at present — and we belong to these — and on the other hand there are the excarnated human beings, the ones who are just now in a body-free condition. All the people who have died are still people! And they will continue to be so, with the one difference that at the moment they have no physical bodies. So if we are looking at the sum total of human beings we have to add the number of excarnated souls to the number of souls on earth. And when we add them all together the number is always the same. In other words, when the world population increases the population in heaven decreases accordingly. Apart from that, the absolute number of excarnated human beings is always higher than the number of incarnated ones, because a person normally spends much longer in the spiritual world than in the physical.

The reason why there have been more human beings in incarnation in recent times than a century or so ago is, from the point of view of reincarnation, the simplest one imaginable. As you know, people are living longer and longer these days; they remain on the earth longer, grow older and older, and when they die they have behind them a life of materialism. Consequently, after their death they take with them into the spiritual world a stronger desire for the material world, and therefore they are less able to get their bearings and are less open to things of the spirit. This is why in recent times human beings have acquired the tendency to return a little sooner.

Without these perspectives of reincarnation there is no explaining the 'population explosion'. One would have to state God's reason for 'creating' considerably more human beings today than in bygone times. Or one would explain the increase by means of 'chance'. Things could of course change to the extent humankind succeeds in transcending this materialistic phase, which means overcoming it. However, this phase is also part of evolution, as we said before, and every human being has to go through this needle's eye of materialism.

Materialism can indeed be compared to an eye of a needle that the human being has to pass through. In going through it he loses or, in this case, forgets everything he knew — to the extent that he sometimes does not have the faintest awareness any more that there is such a thing as the spiritual world. In the course of our evolution each one of us has to reach the point where we have no conception any longer of the spiritual world, not even one based on tradition or soul sentiment. So that when an awareness of it arises again in the future each single human being will aspire to it in freedom, and it will no longer arise out of atavistic clairvoyance, tradition or mortal fear, but out of an independent, conscious search for knowledge.

According to the findings of spiritual science materialism is a stage of evolution like any other, and therefore just as necessary as the others. To be precise, the stage of materialism is necessary for the ego to acquire freedom. An essential ingredient of materialism is our so-called rational, abstract thinking. Everybody has to learn to think scientifically and to develop an enquiring mind and, in the course of so doing, lose sight of the spiritual world and its living realities for a while!

Each human being must spend in the course of his evolution at least one incarnation in which abstract thinking plays a major role. There are specific experiences and evolutionary steps which can only be accomplished thanks to exercising and eventually overcoming abstract thinking. There is only one way of overcoming abstract rationalism and materialism: you must go through it and make it your own. You cannot overcome it unless you have first of all made it your own. The stages of evolution are of such a nature that they cannot be skipped. Each human being must go through all the stages.

Now let us take a look at the essentials of what each human being, according to Rudolf Steiner, experiences between death and a new birth. Immediately after death, for a period of three to three and a half days, the human being sees his whole past life in imaginative pictures. He has laid aside his physical body, and now for the first time his etheric body, his life forces, have separated from his physical body. That is what death is.

Every night the ego, that is, the spirit, and also the astral body, the person's soul, leave the physical body. But the etheric body, also called life body or body of formative forces, remains in the physical body; therefore during sleep — death's little brother — a human being does not die.

At death not only the ego and astral body (that is, spirit and soul) leave the physical body, but also the etheric body or life forces. This means that the chemical forces of dissolution and decomposition now deal with the physical body in the way they deal with lifeless matter. For three to three and a half days—about as long as one can normally remain awake in life—the deceased sees, by means of the forces of his etheric body, the whole of his life in the form of a gigantic panorama.

After this short span of time the etheric body now yields to the inclination it felt directly on being released from the physical body to spread out into space, reach out into the expanses of the cosmos. This is why the vast memory tableau, containing all the details of a person's life, disappears after three days. Now the human being begins no longer to live in the imaginative picture world of his etheric body but in his astral body. The human being then lives in the world of the soul. What does he now experience in his soul? Not the things he experienced consciously in life, for those have already been dealt with, but the things within him of which he was not previously conscious. We could also say that the human being is now in 'purgatory' or in 'kamaloka', as it is called in Sanskrit. (Sanskrit *loka*, Latin *locus*, Engl. *locality*. The Sanskrit word *kama* is rendered best in English as 'passion' or 'burning desire'; the Greek word *gamos* = 'a matrimonial union', for instance, is also derived from this. In the realm of sexuality we have the greatest amount of passion. There are many words, also in other languages, which are derived from this Sanskrit word.) So purgatory or kamaloka is the 'abode of passion', the 'place of burning desire', where human beings now dwell and where they now encounter consciously everything their souls were previously involved with but of which they could not then become conscious. In purgatory a human being has, on the one hand, to break himself of body-based habits and, on the other hand, to acquire soul experiences with which he was not previously acquainted.

What do I have in my soul during life of which I am not conscious? During earth life I experience only those occurrences consciously which I sense directly with my astral body, and these are the things which make up the egoistic part of my soul. But in my astral body all those things have also taken up habitation which I have done to others; this returns to my astral body, but I am unconscious of it. This is why, after the human being has for three days seen the memory tableau with the forces of his etheric body, he has to spend a certain time in purgatory, in kamaloka, so that he can be made conscious of what he was previously unconscious. The duration of this time is about a third of his lifetime, which is the time he spent sleeping in his earthly life. So if a person dies at the age of 90 he will stay in kamaloka for about 30 years.

In kamaloka we live through our life once again but in reverse order, and go through all we experienced at night but of which we were then unconscious. Being in kamaloka means, in other words, experiencing one's life once again, backwards, this time not the life we experienced during the day but the night-time experiences.

What do we mean by 'day'? When we say day we are referring to the events we were consciously involved in. When we say 'night' we mean all those things we experienced unconsciously. So in kamaloka we have to live through our nights once more, this time consciously. We have to have a conscious soul experience of the pleasure or pain we gave to others. The joy another person felt because I gave him words of encouragement I now feel myself; it becomes part of myself because it was I who caused it. Similarly I also experience in myself the pain another suffered because I spoke discouraging words to him, and only saw his negative side; and this pain, too, becomes part of me.

Thus during the three days we view the memory tableau we are seeing the day aspect of our last earth life, and after that, in purgatory, in kamaloka, we are concerned during a period of time corresponding to a third of our lifetime with the night experiences of our last life. During the first three days we see things in the nature of pictures, whereas in kamaloka we live through soul experiences and experience in ourselves what others have experienced because of us.

However, human beings still have within them in their astral body, in their soul, all the longings and desires which they were able to satisfy solely by means of their physical body. Initially these longings are still there after death. A further characteristic of the life in kamaloka now consists in a person having to get used to not being able to satisfy these longings any longer. This puts him 'on fire' again to such an extent that the familiar picture of the red-hot flames is definitely a very suitable image for purgatory. Imagine a gourmet who enjoys nothing better than good food and a glass of the best wine suddenly finding himself in a desert where day after day he gets nothing to eat or drink. What does he go through? He feels deprived. This experience, however, is just like a red-hot flame consuming his desire. His longings can no longer be satisfied, so they wear themselves out; they are attacked by flames and burnt out until they have completely gone.

This time span, this period lasting as long as a third of life, when a person is preoccupied with himself, is a period of soul activity. The human being lives in his soul. He certainly begins to connect with other people with whom he has a karmic link, but everything he experiences in kamaloka in relation to others is experienced as a purification of his own soul. In another context Rudolf Steiner also calls this realm the 'moon-sphere'. It is characteristic of this moon-sphere that while a human being is there he has not yet risen to the spirit. For spirit signifies objectivity, and as long as I am occupied with my personal life of soul I am still in the subjective realm.

The so-called dead person therefore lives initially in this third of his lifetime in a world of subjectivity. As we have said, the goal of this phase is purification. Then everything karmic, everything of a purely subjective nature, all that is of purely personal concern to a human being is then left behind in this 'moon-sphere'. And when the person is able to function later on at a universally objective level, this is solely because he was permitted to leave behind him what Steiner calls his 'karmic package'. If he had to continue to take his subjective karma, the karma of his personal life, with him, his experiences in the spiritual world, which he reaches when he enters the 'sun-sphere', would be dulled, and he would not be able to see and experience the objective reality of the spiritual worlds.

So the transition after death from the moon-sphere to the sun-sphere is none other than the step (and what a mighty one it is!) from subjective to objective experience — from the soul to the spirit realm.

However, between the moon and the sun there are two intermediary worlds: the Mercury-sphere and the Venus-sphere. In the moon-sphere we are concerned, as we said, with everything of a purely personal nature. Now, in the Mercury-sphere, human beings are involved with moral impulses and in the Venus-sphere with religious impulses.

Indeed, morality and religion are two realities which are able to help human beings to become all-embracing and objective, for what is morally good or bad is not a question of preference or liking. That which is worthy of being revered from a religious point of view — God, for example — does not belong to race, nation or blood relationship. These two intermediary stages, that of moral life and religious life, are situated between the moon and the sun because human beings, particularly in pre-Christian times, were not yet in a position to find the universally objective dimension in either the moral or the religious sphere, for they did not as yet possess the necessary ego force.

The fact that until today we still have different religious confessions existing side by side in the world and, as it were, mutually excluding one another, means that the religious life is still in need of further development. For true religiousness is a relation to the objective spiritual world and its beings. In this area total unity and harmony should prevail among humankind. At present, however, we are only at the beginning of the process of becoming universal. Human beings consciously reach the sun-sphere — which is the sphere of the Christ, for the word 'Christ' signifies the universal being of the sun — to the extent that they attain the level of universality and individuality.

Everything to do with group nature has been given us so that we can overcome it. And in this context a group does not only mean a party, a firm or a family. A group also covers the particular religion I belong to, and with which I at the same time express the fact that I do *not* belong to the 'other' religions. In this sense religion is also a group, for it is neither universal nor individual. Just as we are confronted with nature so that we can redeem and transform it according to the law of freedom, we are also confronted with the mystery of group nature within which human beings are not yet individual nor universal. We also have to overcome this, so that each one of us can realize and experience his or her dignity as a human being in an individual and independent way, a way that is at the same time applicable to all human beings and yet wholly unique.

These two dimensions, universality on the one hand and individuality on the other, could not be grasped before death by earthly humanity prior to the incarnation of Christ. People could not experience these things within themselves prior to the coming of Christ for they still belonged together in groups. It was the Christ Event which once and for all brought down onto the earth the universally human ego forces, and it is now the ego force of each one of us which will enable us to become both universally human and uniquely individual at one and the same time.

An example of the fact that pre-Christian evolution was of a group nature can be seen in the civilization of the Hebrew people which in its later period had the task of preparing for the birth of Jesus of Nazareth into whom the Christ later entered. The prophets always maintained that it was a preparation for the time when the coming of the Messiah would bring both individuality and universality. They were little understood, however, just because the period was pre-Christian. In other words, human beings begin to live as 'Christians' to the extent they enter the dimension of universality and individuality. To the extent a person has not entered this dimension he still lives as a 'pre-Christian', he lives in the Old Testament, even though 2000 years have elapsed since Christ's ministry.

The Christ came to earth especially to enable us to have on the earth this double experience of universality and individuality. This implies that life after death was quite different for human beings before the Christ Event than afterwards. For before the Mystery of Golgotha a human being died as a Hindu or a Buddhist or a Jew — and not simply as a human being and an individual. In that epoch a human being did not encounter the Sun Being of Christ until after death as he entered the sun-sphere at the end of kamaloka, for Christ was still in the sun-sphere and not on the earth as He is today. And only then did the Christ enable him to be conscious of this totally different dimension beyond everything of a group nature, and lead him into the mysteries of what is objective, universal and individual. Since His appearance on earth we are, after death, no longer accompanied by the Christ when we pass from the moon to the sun-sphere, for the Christ is no longer on the sun.

Since the Christ Event, therefore, our ability to rise from the moon to the sun-sphere depends on how far we have succeeded *during our life on earth* in reaching the level of awareness enabling us to have a conscious, independent, living meeting with the Christ Being. It does not matter whether we actually call this Being the 'Christ' or not. The name is not important.

A person who has both an awareness of what we human beings have in common and an awareness of the uniqueness of each individual human being is a 'Christian'. It does not matter whether he was born a Buddhist or lives in the Hindu or Islamic world. And a person who has little or no awareness of these two dimensions of a human being is not a Christian, even if he was born in a 'Christian' country and was baptized a 'Christian'. Each one of us is called upon to meet the Representative of Humankind during our life on earth—and since the Mystery of Golgotha this is now the one and only possibility of doing so.

When, after death, we have reached the objective sphere of the cosmos we continue further until, beyond the sun-sphere, we come to the mysteries of Mars, Jupiter and Saturn. When a human being enters the Saturn-sphere he experiences what Steiner calls the 'midnight hour of existence'. The 'cosmic midday' of our life occurs around the thirty-fifth year, when we are at the prime of life on earth. We experience the 'cosmic midnight' when we reach the summit of the path leading us higher and higher into the objective reality of the cosmos. Then the descent begins towards a new earth life.

Before this change of direction occurs and the descent begins, that is, until the 'cosmic midnight' of his cosmic life, the human being becomes more and more a cosmos himself; he has stripped off all his soul attributes and also left his karma behind. Now the point has come when the human being wants to reincarnate; the wish for a new existence arises in him. The word existence comes from

Latin from the verb *exsistere*, which as good as means 'departing from'. Accordingly, to harbour the wish for a new existence means to want to end the universal communion with the cosmos in which, at the present stage of evolution, the human being still loses his individuality in a certain way. Thus the desire for a physical body reappears, and in this phase the human being prepares what Rudolf Steiner calls the 'spirit germ' of his future body. The whole objective world and the world of the individual weave together the forces the human being will need in order to clothe himself again in a physical body.

Here again Steiner describes the descent in three consecutive phases. One phase is during the cosmic midnight, when the human ego interrelates with the divine beings themselves. Then comes a phase when the consciousness of the ego is dimmed, which means a phase in which the human being can no longer distinguish these beings one from another, and experiences solely their revelations. It is in this phase that the ego again acquires an interest in the earth and that the longing reawakens to re-enter a physical body. This longing grows stronger and stronger with time, and now the I begins to be on the look-out for certain successive generations of lives on earth. Each of us before we incarnate is involved in forming series of generations as far back as the thirty-sixth generation. If we reckon about three generations to a century we realize for how long a period of time we take part in the shaping of humanity of earth!

Now the feeling of being an individual self awakens, something which was not there before because the human being was totally embedded in the objective reality of the cosmos. There is a noticeable reawakening of interest in the historical development of humankind on the earth, and finally the transition from the sun to the moon-sphere occurs. In the moon-sphere, which as already mentioned is the sphere of the soul, the human being picks up his karma again — the 'karmic package' he had left behind, which is a kind of extract of his earlier karma — and clads himself in it. His feeling of self becomes stronger and stronger, and the human being grows more and more into a being of soul (previously he was spirit only), until in the process of incarnating, at the moment of conception, he loses the spiritual germ of the physical body. This world of spiritual forces engaged in forming the physical body escapes from him.

The human being, who is still in the spiritual world, experiences this moment as a tremendous loss. Up till now he was first of all a spiritual ego, then he became an astral body who had taken his whole karma upon himself, and there with him was the most precious and godlike thing he could ever have, and which for centuries he had worked with the spiritual Hierarchies to create: the spiritual germ of the physical body — free of matter. Now it had gone astray! Where had it gone?

The spiritual germ of the physical body, this 'phantom', a sum of the formative forces of the physical body, has descended to the earth and combined with the fertilized ovum in the mother's womb. While the human being is still in the spiritual world it now begins to work on the embryo.

This feeling of painful loss causes the human being to gather those forces from out of the world of cosmic ether which he needs to form his own etheric body. He clads himself in an etheric body, a body of life forces. And this is the third phase a human being experiences as he descends to a new earthly life. The etheric body is formed out of the cosmic ether after the germ of the physical body has already entered the maternal womb and is applying its forces to building up the physical body which is beginning to take shape.

About the seventeenth day after conception — this period varies according to the stage of development of the human individuality — that is, in about the third week, the ego, astral body and etheric body unite with the spiritual germ of the physical body, and from this moment on there comes about the tremendously important direct participation of the ego in the development of the embryo in the body of the mother.

This is the beginning of a very complex process, namely, the increasing mutual interpenetration of the etheric body, astral body and ego with matter. We can see for instance in the uncoordinated movements of a newly born baby that the ego has not yet fully descended into matter. There are complex processes at work here, and these take place step by step.

Just as a human being before birth first of all lives for a while in the company of individual spiritual beings, then experiences the cosmic Word in a more general way, and finally passes through the etheric world where he takes up the forces of life and growth which will maintain the life of his physical body throughout the whole of earth life, we see similarly in the development of the little child three pronounced phases that are a kind of mirror picture of these three sublime prenatal stages.

The first is the phase of standing upright and learning to walk. Rudolf Steiner draws our attention to the fact that in learning to orientate himself as a vertical being in the cosmos and in learning to walk wherever he wants to go and wherever his karma calls him, the child masters whole worlds. The development a child undergoes when he learns to orient himself and learns to distinguish between different directions and decide which one to choose is absolutely tremendous. The phase of standing upright and learning to walk is of the nature of an earthly repetition of the first phase we spoke of above, the phase in which the ego lived in communion with spiritual beings; for communion with spiritual beings is the highest form of orientation, the highest form of following a path.

The phase of learning to speak, the phase of the Word, corresponds to the second prenatal phase, the one in which we perceived the revelations and the mutual relationships of the spiritual beings, in which we no longer recognized the spiritual beings themselves individually but experienced now only the universal 'Cosmic Word', the Logos.

The third prenatal phase, in which the human being clads himself in the ether forces of the cosmos to build his etheric body, is mirrored in the capacity to think which develops in the third pronounced developmental phase. For the capacity to think is the capacity to connect oneself to the life forces of the cosmos and to move spiritually according to the laws of its transformations.

Lecture 3

ARE THERE INDICATIONS OF REINCARNATION IN THE GOSPELS?
The Christ Event and Repeated Earth Lives

If it is true that human beings live more than once, and if this is not a matter of secondary importance but on the contrary a fact of decisive significance, then every human being who calls himself a Christian will be extremely interested in finding out what the Gospels have to say concerning this important theme.

The first train of thought we might follow is this. If we were in a position to point out that in the Gospels there are statements that clearly and distinctly speak against reincarnation, then Rudolf Steiner's spiritual science would be in a difficult if not hopeless situation, for the very reason that Rudolf Steiner regards the Gospels as texts written by initiates and which therefore can only contain the truth. There are, however, no such statements in them. But so that you will not think I am concealing anything I will tell you straight away that in the Epistle to the Hebrews there is a passage which runs: 'And as it is appointed unto men once to die, but after this the judgment: So Christ was once offered to bear the sins of many ...' (Hebrews 9:27, 28) This sentence is often quoted as a statement refuting reincarnation. Yet it is the only one to be found in this connection. Anyone hearing or reading it ought, however, to ask himself the following. If the intention of Holy Scripture is to prove that reincarnation is *not a fact*, why does it contain nothing more on this most important theme than this one short sentence?

Apart from this, in the instances when this sentence is quoted people do not take into consideration that nowhere in the whole of the ninth chapter of the Epistle to the Hebrews is reincarnation under discussion. The question as to whether a human being lives once or more than once is answered neither positively nor negatively in the ninth chapter of the Epistle to the Hebrews, for the question is not even raised! All that is said is that the human being dies only once. And I ask you: even if a person were to live more than once, how many times in each life would he die? Only once each time!

If the question as to whether a person lives once or more than once were unmistakably the theme of the ninth chapter of the Epistle to the Hebrews then we could very well consider this sentence the answer to the question. But this question is not the theme of this chapter of the Epistle to the Hebrews. Therefore it is inadmissible to try and prove anything in this direction by tearing this sentence out of its context where it obviously applies to each single life. Even if we had a hundred lives we would only die once in each one of them and not several times.

However, the fact that nothing is said against reincarnation in the New Testament does not automatically mean that anything is being said in its favour.

Over and over again someone will up and maintain that reincarnation is quite clearly mentioned in the Gospels. This is not so. The Christians of earlier generations would all have been very stupid if they had not noticed something stated clearly in Holy Scripture. In no way can we say that reincarnation is spoken of in the Gospels so plainly that everyone can see it, or that the Gospels clearly confirm reincarnation. What is far more characteristic of the Gospels is that the mystery of reincarnation is alluded to in a more indirect way.

Rudolf Steiner represents the view that the fact of rein-carnation is expressed in the Gospels in a somewhat hidden

form. In other words, you only discover it if you approach
Holy Scripture with a certain openness of mind.

Until a human being has awakened, through inner
struggle, to certain forces of thought and problems of
knowledge there will be things in the Gospels he will not be
able to see and understand. But being close to the threshold
as we now are, the time has come when just these powers of
knowledge are beginning to awaken, and people are starting to approach Holy Scripture with just those particular
questions and capacities of heart and mind which lead them
to things which earlier generations did not notice.

Besides, those earlier generations, the people living a
thousand or two thousand years ago, were actually ourselves, if reincarnation applies. So we can be grateful that
today we are in a position to approach Holy Scripture with
new questions, and to discover what we could not discover
centuries ago.

The best way I can illustrate this is to give a concrete
example from my own life. In a great many conversations
with Catholic priests — people with a well-established basis
of theological knowledge — I have referred to the beginning
of the ninth chapter of the St John's Gospel, where it speaks
of the man born blind. 'Does it not strike you as peculiar,' I
asked them, 'that the apostles themselves, and not just
anybody, ask the Christ: "Who did sin, this man, or his
parents, that he was born blind?" Don't you think this is
strange?' And every time the answer was 'No!' So I read the
passage to them again. The third time I did so I emphasized
the words '*he* or his parents', and repeated '*he*' once more,
adding: 'He was not even born then!' — 'You are right,'
almost every one of them concluded at this point, 'I never
noticed that before!'

The decisive factor is whether each individual today
approaches Holy Scripture with certain questions; for then
we shall be alert to these things. Generally speaking theo-
logians have not given much thought to this sentence up till

now, and have not tried to get to the bottom of it and to understand what the apostles meant by it. They have hardly been aware that the apostles are asking whether the man is born blind because he himself has sinned.

Anyone who asks a question of that sort is certainly assuming that, at the least, we have a prenatal life. This does not mean that we can assume that this question indicates a definite confirmation of reincarnation. But without doubt there is inherent in the question the assumption that this person already existed before birth and therefore could be to blame for his blindness.

According to Rudolf Steiner it was actually the task of Christ, initially, to withhold from humanity the ancient knowledge of reincarnation for a while. During these 2000 years of Christianity the West has indeed lost the pre-Christian consciousness of reincarnation — and this is due to the very deed of Christ! For the Christ came to give humanity the chance of forgetting all they once knew by virtue of the ancient atavistic clairvoyance they all possessed. Why? Because the type of consciousness of reincarnation that the people had before Christ had not arisen out of their own individual thought process, and was not their own independently acquired knowledge, but was a kind of echo, the last and usually not very well-interpreted remainder of the ancient 'automatic' atavistic clairvoyance. We can see this in the fact that the apostles were not actually clear about what their question comprised.

John the Baptist also does not know that he is Elias, as is plainly reported in the Gospels. For when he is asked 'Are you Elias?' he answers, 'No, I am not' (John 1:21). His consciousness of reincarnation has been eclipsed, and he no longer knows who he was in his previous life — which does not mean that he was not actually Elias.

Christ's ministry extinguished the consciousness of reincarnation in its ancient form because this lacked the two dimensions that are of decisive importance for *Christian* evolution, meaning the evolution of the free ego, namely, the individual and the universal dimension.

All the ancient forms of a *consciousness* of reincarnation have thus to be lost so that a *new consciousness* of reincarnation can arise, the consciousness that all human beings belong together as members of a single organism. And just as we needed the first half of evolution to evolve away from one another, to become independent beings, each one an individual in him or herself, we now need the second half with all its incarnations to grow together again, to become *one* organism together, without losing the consciousness of our individuality in the process.

We have passed through two successive phases of evolution (and when we look at the development of a little child we can observe that the same phases are repeated in each single human life). First came the state of original paradisaical unity without any division or differentiation, or any separate independence as individuals; then came the phase of splitting up and losing our connection, the phase we are in today and which will continue for a long time to come. It is the goal of our evolution to bring together these dimensions we lived through one after the other, and experience them simultaneously.

Therefore, from the Christian point of view, reincarnation means evolving towards the goal of building the body of Christ in the course of the millennia out of the forces of the free resolve and co-operation of every single human being, thus bringing about a togetherness of all people, a universal human organism in which, however, each single person remains an individual.

Christ's answer to the apostles' question 'Who did sin, this man or his parents, that he was born blind?' is even more difficult to interpret. The traditional translation says: 'Neither hath this man sinned nor his parents: but that the works of God should be made manifest in him.' Christ's answer is normally interpreted to mean that God made him to be born blind so that He could give him sight later, and thus show through him His working.

To this Steiner says that nobody with a healthy religious feeling can be satisfied with this translation. As though the fact that God makes the sun to rise and set every day and, every spring anew, makes the earth to glow in an infinite variety of wonderful colours, and gives us children who smile at us with *seeing* eyes — as though all these wonders were not enough to testify to His great works!

Let us have a look at the Greek text (John 9:3) and translate it literally, yet with the help of spiritual science: 'Neither this man [i.e. the man he is in this life] has sinned nor his parents, but that there should be made manifest the works of the God in him.'

The God-in-him, however, is the ego! The Greek text speaks of the godlike being *in* himself, i.e. which is he himself, and not of the general Godhead, which works on him from outside as it were. For the concept *Theos* in the New Testament is not identical with the concept which became established in theology later on, and which refers only to *the* God, that is, to a single God. In the New Testament a variety of beings are described as 'God' or 'divine beings', for example the Hierarchies. And in the tenth chapter of the St John's Gospel Christ himself says with reference to human beings: 'Ye are gods — *Theoi este*' (John 10:34). This statement presents theology with another big problem.

So Christ's answer is: 'The godlike being in him', the eternal individuality of this human being, his ego, has done something in a past life which has to be balanced; hence the resolve to enter the world blind in this life.

It is a free resolve made by the godlike ego in himself, please note, and not a punishment. For karma has nothing to do with punishment. Taking one's karma upon oneself always means being thankful that one is permitted to compensate for one's one-sidedness in the course of one's further positive development. This is quite different from serving a sentence – it is the exact opposite. The higher ego, the godlike being in this human being, has in freedom and thankfulness accepted the grace which offers him the opportunity to come into the world blind, to be able to balance what has to be balanced for the future good of his higher being. Each karmic compensation is a chance to acquire ever new aspects of being human. The higher self is especially thankful for possibilities of suffering – for instance being blind – because they offer the greatest possibility of growth.

According to Rudolf Steiner the fundamental law underlying reincarnation is that what in one life is inside, that is, in the soul and the spirit, cannot in the same life perpetually transform the bodily sheaths. For at the present stage of evolution the body is highly impermeable. So even if a radical transformation takes place in the astral body and ego the physical body cannot at the same time be correspondingly transformed. The change the ego brings about, the inner change that occurs in this life, does not come to expression in the body until the following life. It is precipitated in a kind of extract which the human being forms from the totality of the inner development of a lifetime, and takes it with him from this life into the next to form his new body with.

Just because we are not capable in one and the same lifetime of changing the basic characteristics of our body, it is not until the next life that we are given the opportunity to build up a new body in the image of what we have inwardly become. The whole point of death and new birth is that *because* during each lifetime a greater and greater discrepancy is *bound to* arise between the inner life, which is capable of infinite development, and the natural inertia of the body the human being has to lay aside the body, which is no longer suitable, in order to construct a new one corresponding to his new level of development.

A great deal could still be said with regard to the man born blind. However, the important thing in this context is to emphasize that this narrative does in fact contain a reference to reincarnation, and that this reference is only obvious to a person if he is able to understand that the man was born blind because blindness allowed him to make the particular kind of progress he had resolved to make. Blindness is the karmic consequence of the previous life of this human being. This body with its blindness is essential so that he can take the next steps in his further development. This chance of being born blind is afforded him by grace, and prior to his birth he consciously and thankfully accepts this grace, this opportunity, because he realizes that good can come of it.

In the previous chapter, the eighth, where it speaks of the adulteress, we have a case which, in a way, is the opposite. In the story of the man born blind our gaze is directed to the past; we understand that this man's bodily nature in this life is the result of the inner path he followed in a previous life. The story of the adulteress, on the other hand, tells us about a person who does something in this life which will affect her next life.

We must not consider the adulteress solely as a real individual woman, but at the same time as a common image of every human soul. And because the picture of the soul is always feminine the story is about a woman.

This woman stands for every human soul, and in the course of evolution souls in general have behaved like adulteresses. We must realize that the only way to become free, become individual egos separated from one another, was by descending deeper and deeper into matter. The path the human soul has been and still is pursuing is therefore inevitably a path of disloyalty—disloyalty towards the primeval spirit. The human soul deserts her first 'husband', the spirit, becomes a cosmic adulteress and gives herself to a second 'husband', the body.

That is the great 'adultery' which the course of evolution has demanded. That is Original Sin. It is the expulsion from Paradise. The soul becomes unfaithful to the spirit — 'severs' itself from it through Original Sin — to give itself to the body, to enter into marriage with matter. The word sin is akin to sunder: it is the fragmenting of humanity due to the descent into matter.

What Moses wanted to convey through his law was as follows. Through this adultery demanded by evolution the human soul becomes unfaithful to the spirit and connects itself with the body, with matter. It thus forges a link with the realm of dead mineral matter, with the 'stones' — and it is these stones which bring about its downfall. In his union with natural necessity the human being is pelted with stones, which means he is lost and, as a free being, dead. This evolutionary adultery leads the human being to lose himself in the mineral world, kill himself. Moses is saying: You should look on the person who abandons himself to the instinctive desires of natural necessity, and who thereby loses his freedom, as humanly 'dead'; you should think of him as 'dead'. It is his task to arise again through the power of his own freedom.

Later, Moses was understood to have said: Kill him physically with stones. Therefore the question is put to Christ: 'But what sayest thou? Shall we stone her or not?' They think they are setting a trap for Christ, to put Him to the test. For if He were to tell them they should not stone the adulteress, they could say: 'So you speak against the law of Moses.' However, if He were to say, 'Yes, stone her,' then they could reply, 'So you are also in favour of killing a person solely because she has committed adultery.'

But Christ stooped down and with His finger wrote on the ground. From the viewpoint of reincarnation this is a deed of the greatest significance. Christ, writing on the body of the earth, engraving the deeds of human beings on the earth body, is showing that He Himself is making the earth into His body and taking all our deeds upon Himself. His gesture says: It is totally unnecessary to pass a hasty judgment on the woman; human beings do not need to put one another on immediate trial, for each one of us, on returning to earth, finds his deeds waiting for him.

The mystery of reincarnation is being referred to in a delicate way, although to anyone able to understand it it is quite clear. The indication is there that each one of us keeps returning to the earth, and that human beings do not need blindly to judge and kill one another, because the justice of karma, working throughout all our earth lives, is a justice based on love.

Let us now leave these individual examples we have found in the Gospels and turn to the Christ Event in its totality, in its essential all-embracing significance. A completely different perspective opens up. By taking reincarnation into account we arrive at an altogether new interpretation of Christianity. Fundamentally there are two possible ways of understanding the Christ Event. There is a kind of Christianity that so to speak puts a bracket round human freedom, and there is a kind of Christianity that underlines freedom.

Up till now humanity has basically got to know only the first kind. Christ's words and deeds, that is, what Christ said and did, have up till now been understood more from the point of view of grace and less from the point of view of freedom. This has brought it about that grace and freedom have been considered to be opposites. The words of Christ have been 'dogmatized' in that human beings have been told: There are many things you cannot understand – the important thing is that you believe them. By demanding that people should believe the words of Christ without grasping them in thought, the mystery of freedom has in a sense been put in brackets. Initially, in the first phase of Christianity, nothing else was possible. The dogmas arising

in this way had first of all to be taken up more in the form of
forbidden thoughts rather than thoughts they were
encouraged to think in the interests of the further creative
development of the human spirit.

The second and even more important dimension of the
Gospel, the deeds of Christ, were understood to be 'miracles'. And when people said that the Christ performed
miracles they meant that Christ performed godlike and not
human deeds. They denied the human being a godlike part
on principle, for by definition a human being is human and
not godlike. They said: 'As Christ is a godlike being, so are
His deeds godlike, and with His deeds He is showing us
what He can do which we cannot.'

Rudolf Steiner's spiritual science radically questions this
way of interpreting Christianity.

When Christ, with His so-called miracles, performs deeds
which a human being could never do, such as the raising of
Lazarus or the healing of the man born blind, His very
incarnation as a *human being* is radically questioned. When
Christ came to earth He was tempted by the devil especially
for the purpose of finding out whether He had become fully
human. For with the words, 'You can do what no man can
do, demonstrate to human beings what is humanly
impossible, change stones into bread!' the devil was of
course endeavouring to tempt Jesus.

The traditional interpretation of the Gospels does in fact
go in the direction of describing Christ as though He suc-
cumbs to these temptations all the time, and is prepared to
show human beings what He alone, as a godlike being, can
accomplish!

However, the answer Christ gives the tempter is in this
vein: Devil, I know I could do what no human being can do,
but you must know that my decision to become *man* consists in renouncing everything that is humanly impossible,
and keeping strictly to what is within the bounds of
possibility for humans to do—if not at the *present* stage of

their evolution, at least within the evolutionary prospects of human potential.

What would it signify for our human dignity if a divine being were constantly to show us things which, in principle, we could not do? If we wanted to call that love, love *for human beings*, we would be hugely mistaken. For whoever loves another being tries to help him develop his own capacities, and does not do something instead of him in order to humiliate him.

According to Rudolf Steiner all Christ's deeds, including the resurrection, are within the bounds of the humanly possible. Including the resurrection! This is recognizing the divine stage of existence as a dimension of the possible evolution of every human being.

But what do the words and deeds of Christ have to do with reincarnation? Why am I speaking here at all of the words and deeds of Christ?

If we understand all that the Christ carried out to be the real and possible goal of what we human beings are called upon to become, then it is clear we must have several lives available.

If we say that human beings have the opportunity, in a real sense, to realize in themselves all those dimensions seen in the incarnated Christ, we must also say that they will need many lives in which to do it. For example, they need a number of lives in order to acquire the spiritual strength necessary to spiritualize matter. For this is exactly what the task of resurrection is. For the resurrection body is the greatest spiritual force of transformation of matter, the redemption of matter, out of the necessity of nature, of determinism, for creating a spiritual body according to the law of the free spirit. It is a body that gives human beings a way of expressing themselves outwardly in total harmony with the inner law, that of love and freedom. If human beings had only *one* life — the present one — at their disposal, the distance between God and humanity would remain in principle unbridgeable. The state in which *every* human being — even the 'best' — dies today is infinitely far away from a real and lasting deification. Thus a loss of an awareness of reincarnation had of necessity to lead to the one-sided stress of the 'transcendence' of God, that is, of the absolute dissimilarity, in principle, between God and mankind.

In the course of our development over the coming centuries each one of us — in the perspective of reincarnation — will be summoned to decide between the one kind of Christianity and the other: the kind in which the Christ performs miracles in the sense that He does things for human beings that are His accomplishments and *not* human accomplishments, and the other kind in which the Christ shows human beings what they themselves are called upon to become.

Rudolf Steiner's spiritual science is quite clear about the fact that Christ demonstrates to us what is humanly possible and not what is humanly impossible. This is why, in the St John's Gospel, the so-called miracles are called demonstrations or 'signs'.

Looking at it from the viewpoint of reincarnation, Christ performed all those things human beings will be able to do in the future. Christ's actions contain all that human beings can become capable of achieving, and His words all that human beings can become capable of thinking.

Every word of Christ is a challenge to human thinking. The Logos, the cosmic Word, always expresses the universal law of becoming, not in the sense that we must believe it without understanding it but in the sense that the words of Christ contain all the tasks that human beings in the course of their development (obviously not in one single life) have to solve by means of their thinking.

Christ is the being of love solely because He has made Himself the real and attainable ideal of human freedom.

We live in a world in which there is nature and bodily

nature. In nature we have the universal potential for thinking, for human beings can think about what is sense-perceptible. And we live in the field of karmic connections, in the world of the soul, where we experience the individual potential for action.

On the one side Christ gives us the mystery of nature, which contains everything the human being can think; herein lies the universal task for all of us. And on the other side Christ gives each one of us the mystery of his own karma, which contains everything the individual can do. However, on every hand we meet with dimensions of evolving freedom, in one case with the unfolding of thinking in freedom and in the other case with the unfolding of will in freedom. Understood in this totally different way Christianity throws a completely new light on some of the utterances made in the Gospels that are basically not understood in traditional interpretations, for example the already quoted 'Ye are gods' (John 10:34).

A further example belonging here are the words which come again and again in the Gospels, especially the synoptic ones: '*Thy* faith has made thee whole.' We always find these words in the places where we would say that Christ Himself has performed a miracle. But what actually happened? Did Christ perform the miracle, or was the human person decisive for the fact that a miracle had taken place? Christ stresses every time that the deciding factor for a 'miracle' to come about is not His deed but the conditions of inner growth in each single person—therefore not everyone can be healed.

If the necessary conditions hold good, then particular things can happen. '*Thy faith* has made thee whole.' The Greek *pistis* (translated by 'faith') actually means 'on its own foundation'. That is a person's 'salvation', the factor which 'heals' him of all weaknesses.

In his farewell speeches in the fourteenth chapter of the St John's Gospel, Christ says: 'He that believeth on me, the works that I do shall he do also; and greater works than these shall he do; for I go unto my Father'(14,12). 'You shall do greater works.' Christ speaks these words shortly before His death, after the Last Supper. He has already performed all his 'miracles', yet He says quite clearly: 'You shall do greater works.' And in support of this He adds: 'For I go unto my Father.'

In Steiner's Kassel lectures on the St John's Gospel[1] we are told that 'Father' means the whole of the mineral kingdom. The highest Godhead is the one with the power to penetrate into the lowest kingdom of the cosmos — the kingdom that offers the greatest resistance to the power of the spirit, and which the spirit can least penetrate. Therefore in ancient languages we find the same word, *pater, petra,* for the Father within the Trinity and the world of stones. Thus in ancient languages, as a legacy of primeval wisdom, we still find an awareness of the fact that the spirituality of the Father is not situated in the clouds but in the realm of natural laws, which are so to speak the infrastructure, the essential condition for the whole activity of freedom. And the task of freedom lies essentially in the activity of releasing the world of the Father from the law of determinism.

Thus 'I go unto my Father' means: 'I have come in order to penetrate into the world of dead mineral, to unite myself with death, with the world of the Father, *not to lose myself in it, but to transform it.*' Christ wishes to say: 'I am going to enter into the forces of nature, the forces of the mineral realm; I want to penetrate natural necessity.' And as up till then, that is, in the preceding three years, only the first step had been taken, all the deeds that human beings had witnessed up till then were 'small' works. The *great* works will begin when the spirit of Christ, the spirit of the ego, has become so strong that He enters into nature with His love, penetrates it, redeems and transforms it.

In the first half of evolution the 'small' works were

performed. In the second half, after Christ has filled the mineral kingdom with His ego and made it possible for us to experience human freedom in the mineral kingdom while we are incarnated, we shall be in a position to perform the 'great works' of evolution. In other words, the small works of evolution are those in which the spirit is afraid of matter and would prefer to leave it behind and be released from it; the great works of evolution are those in which the human spirit enters into matter, loves it, redeems and transforms it.

You will do still greater works, for I am going to the Father. In Buddhism also — before Christ — there could only be the small works of evolution, for the human spirit wanted to save itself by withdrawing from matter. Now — thanks to the Christ within every human being, the ego force in every human being — it is possible for us to remain true to the love of the earth and perform the *great* works of evolution.

To go to the Father with and in Christ means to resolve time and again to return to an earthly body, to want to incarnate again and again, to remain with Christ until the end of all time, in order to transform the earth into a 'new' earth. That is the *opus magnum*, the great transubstantiation, the great work of evolution.

Lecture Four

METAMORPHOSES OF LOVE AND HATE IN THREE SUCCESSIVE LIVES

Three people find themselves 'by chance' on the same plane to New York. All three of them come from the same small town where something like an environmental catastrophe has occurred, and therefore they are leaving their homeland and intending to start up afresh in the New World. They are between 30 and 35 years old, roughly in the middle of life, and are hoping to find work in America and be able to build up a new life there. They have the same longings as the emigrants of old, who set their hopes on making their fortune in America. In the plane they begin to tell one another a little of their history. It transpires that one of them is a mechanic, another an artist and the third a banker. What they all have in common is the intention to start up again. On arrival in New York each goes their own way. I do not want to go into great detail here about what each of them did every day. They decided, however, to meet up again in a month to exchange news. And I would like to tell you briefly about this.

On the very day of his arrival the mechanic began to look around. He was the type who only noticed cars. Whenever he saw one it held his attention, and nothing else really mattered. For example, he never even noticed bookshops. He very soon discovered where the garages were. A gesture, a smile, a few words exchanged, and hey presto he had landed a little job. Not that he had earned a lot of money yet, but he had made contact with people in the car repair line, and had great hopes of establishing further contacts and building a new life.

The efforts of the artist had been very different. She had not looked at cars or garages, for they did not interest her. That is obvious! She made enquiries about artists, particularly painters, and had also got to know various people. She too had hopes of extending her acquaintances and slowly building up a basis for a new life.

And the banker? He had his own way of looking around. We do not need to go into great detail. The banker obviously tracked down the banks, for these were what interested him.

What the three had in common was, as we have already said, a new start. Each of them approached it, however, in their own area and their own way. The question we must ask here is obvious. Is it by chance that the mechanic concerns himself with cars again, the banker with banks and money and the artist with colours, paint brushes and pictures? The answer is also obviously: No, it is surely not by chance! Each one of us answers 'no', of course it was not by chance. It would more likely have been a chance thing if the three of them had not looked for an opportunity to resume working with their innate skills.

Regarding a situation of this kind, where there is to be a new start within the course of one lifetime, none of us has any doubts. We all have enough life experience to say that these three people did not go to New York as 'unwritten pages' so to speak, but that they had already acquired a certain form and each of them arrived in New York with a distinctly individual character. The unique reality of each person is not an abstract thing but quite the reverse; it is something very concrete, namely, a totality of an infinite number of abilities, sympathies and antipathies, of things the person likes doing and things he could not care less about.

Rudolf Steiner's spiritual science obviously does not only speak of the ego but also of the astral body, that is, the soul, where we find all these currents of interests, abilities,

passions, likes and dislikes etc. Here is a whole world of
harmonies and disharmonies we cannot deny. Thus each of
our three friends emigrating to New York takes along with
him an absolutely real and individualized inner world, and
when they form a connection with the outer world they do
so with reference to their inner world. These are well-
known facts, of course. Everyone knows of them, and
nobody will question them, I am sure. The concept of
reincarnation, however, is no different! It is exactly what I
have just been saying, only carried a little further.

Their new start in America does not turn our three people
into totally different people. The artist will not suddenly
manage a bank, and the banker will not all of a sudden
become a mechanic. Where the inner life of these people is
concerned we are dealing with absolute continuity and we
do not expect them suddenly to become something quite
different from what in the course of time they have become.
What they have become is the result of an ongoing development; it is something that has slowly and continuously
grown to be what it is, in the course of days and years. It is
made up of qualities and capacities that have become
impressed on their inner being and are now part of it.
Looking at it from outside there is a new beginning, looking
at it from inside there is continuity; and this is the fundamental idea we have to start from to understand reincarnation.

A human being is born. Looked at from outside, a person
appears in the world who was not there before – not in his
external form. Looked at from inside, however, this human
being brings a great deal with him; he brings into the world
with him an inner reality of the most diverse forces. You
could describe them as similar to magnetic forces, which
pull him towards certain persons and things and push him
away from others, all according to which way his inner
being has developed in the course of the millennia. With
some people he will form a relation because something

connects him with them, and there will be people he does not make friends with either because he does not meet them at all or when he meets them they hold no interest for him.

The basic idea of reincarnation is that the human being does not enter the world as an 'unwritten page' but is already formed and defined, because he already has a long history behind him.

If we assume that a person starts his life as a brand new human being it is like saying that the three who emigrated to New York have eradicated their whole inner life and are starting again from scratch both outwardly and inwardly. The absurdity of such a thought was up to now only obvious to people as long as they were focusing on *one* life only. Up till now we have not been in the habit in the West of extending our perspective and realizing that we ought to consider such things with regard to the beginning of each life on earth. If we do this, the resulting questions will be basically similar to those arising when someone makes a new start within a single lifetime. Why, of all people, was this human being born to these parents? Why was he born into a rich and not a poor family? Why does one person have such extraordinary soul or spiritual capacities and not another? Why was this person born in Italy and not in Chile? Why? By chance? If we say 'by chance' it is just as though we were to say that it was by chance that the mechanic, the artist or the banker made the connections they did in New York.

Let us picture to ourselves for a moment how distinctly individual each person's earth life is, and what different conditions attend its beginning. To help us understand that human life does not start from zero Rudolf Steiner drew our attention to the mystery of our *biography* (as instanced in his *Theosophy*). The biography of each human being, that is, his path through life, is totally individual, something that is unique, something not found in animals. The way an animal's life runs its course depends on its particular species and is more or less the same for all the animals of one species. The 'variations' between lions do not arise from an inner difference among lions but from the interaction with outer circumstances.

On the other hand if we look at the course of a human life we realize that each one differs from the other in regard to their inner soul world, and that each human being is a species for himself. This holds good also in the case of two human beings who grow up with the same hereditary or educational circumstances.

If I describe the behaviour of a lion I have at the same time described the behaviour of all lions. You may say, perhaps: All very well, but this lion lives in this environment and that one in another. Indeed, but then it is the environment that is different and not the lions! In each case it is correct to say that when I have understood the nature of one lion I have understood the nature of all lions, because lions as lions are all the same. The outer conditions may vary, but these have nothing to do with the inner constitution of the animal.

When I have understood what is 'human' about a human being, what he has in common with all human beings, I have not yet grasped anything about his individuality! I am right at the starting-point, if I want to understand *this* human being in particular and consider the attributes he does *not* share with others. People do not acquire their uniqueness from their life circumstances but express their uniqueness through the circumstances they choose to have in their life.

People have actually always known that each person is his own species, even if they have not formulated it this way. I discover in the mystery of a person's biography in which way each individual is his own species. And I wonder how this biography came about. Where are the causes to be found?

On the basis of Christianity and the Christ Event I have tried to show that reincarnation and karma are the two basic dimensions of *grace*. For reincarnation (that is, the possibility of returning to earth) and karma (that is, the possibility of further development of our capacities, to live out the mystery of our biography) are given to us as the mighty foundations and conditions for our further spiritual growth. They themselves represent grace.

I have also said that it would be the opposite of grace to understand grace as a substitute for freedom, for that would be a misunderstanding of the innermost core of the human being. Christ's love lies in making us capable to do things and not just in doing things for us. Thus perfect love consists in making the other capable in the sense of making the necessary outer conditions and the inner possibilities of growth available, and at the same time leaving the other free to realize these possibilities himself.

Reincarnation and karma—the former can be seen as the divine grace of the *Father*, the possibility of returning again and again into the physical world; the latter can be seen as the divine grace of the *Son*, of being able to live through all the events and experiences necessary for the growth of our inner soul nature.

Rudolf Steiner distinguishes in this connection between the *cosmic* and the *karmic* consequences of our actions. This distinction is also important for understanding the Christian mystery in connection with reincarnation.

The *cosmic* consequences of our deeds are the objective results that enter the world around us, whereas the *karmic* consequences of what we do are those which affect our own inner being.

Steiner once used a drastic example.[2] One person puts another's eyes out. What are the consequences of this action? There is to start with a whole series of results for the person who perpetrated the deed, for from a moral point of view he has become a different, less perfect person. Rudolf Steiner is saying that the actual deed is only the final conclusion of an infinite number of inner changes, and that all the thoughts, feelings and will impulses which the man had to mobilize before he could commit the deed have turned him inwardly into quite a different person. He has now changed in his ego, in his astral body — which is a world for itself, a world of passions, interests, joys and sorrows — in his etheric body and in a certain way in his physical body too. Those are the *karmic* results, and these present a task for the further exercise of freedom. Nobody else can alter anything of this or take part of it away from the perpetrator. Christ does not want to take anything away in this area, either, for He would immediately be taking away the person's freedom. Each one of us is provided with the possibility of coming to grips with the karmic consequences of our actions. To be free means to be capable of taking upon ourselves the karmic results of our actions. A small child has therefore not yet reached freedom.

There is, however, also a second series of consequences. Assuming the person who was robbed of his sight was a farmer, he will now damage a whole number of trees or other plants because he cannot see. Rudolf Steiner calls these the *cosmic* or objective consequences of a deed. They are the results affecting the world beyond that of the perpetrator. The person who put out the farmer's eyes can hardly alter anything to do with the objective results of his action for he cannot save the trees that have been ruined.

Christ does not undertake anything with regard to the karmic results because these are the very things that become the tasks for our growth and will enable us to find the opportunity to exercise our freedom. Instead of this He takes upon Himself all the *cosmic* results of our actions and brings things into the right channels again, making it possible for the person to work anew at the earth's objective evolutionary factors.

Were Christ not to take these cosmic consequences upon Himself we would by now have done such objective damage to the earth that at the present evolutionary stage we could hardly still live on it. One could perhaps object: What about the miserable ecological conditions we live in today? The answer is that we no doubt bear great responsibility for damaging the environment, but that living conditions on earth would be far worse still were Christ not to 'take upon Himself the sins of the world'.

Many of you will certainly know the passage in the Gospels where John the Baptist points to the being of Christ with the words 'Behold the Lamb of God', which means the being of love 'which taketh away the sin of the world — ten hamartian *tou kosmou*' (John 1:29). Not the sins of karma, not the sins of human beings, not the sins we have within us, no, none of that! They are not called 'the sins of the earth', either, but literally 'the sins of the cosmos'.

The Gospel is very precise when it says 'the Lamb of God', meaning the being of sacrifice and love takes upon himself the *cosmic* consequences of our actions, objective reality, not karma. 'Ten hamartian *tou kosmou*' are words with a precise meaning, yet one can only fully understand them with the help of spiritual science.

When people make the objection that, through putting the emphasis on the responsibility of the individual human being — because he has to take his karma on himself — spiritual science is suggesting that grace is superfluous. We have to reply that this statement is based on a big misunderstanding. For if we were to understand what the Christ does in our cosmos to support the earth on which we live we would be full of thankfulness for all the works of grace, for no single human being is capable of balancing the objective, cosmic consequences of his deeds. Nobody is capable of having even the smallest notion of the immeasurable grace Christ bestows on us by making the earth *His* body and taking *upon Himself* all the objective results of our deeds.

* * *

The distinction of the Godhead into a Trinity—Father, Son and Holy Spirit—is of the greatest importance in Christianity. The mode of activity of the Father is quite different from that of the Son, and the Holy Spirit is different again. The Father, as we mentioned yesterday, has His sphere of activity in the natural workings of our bodily nature. Of what significance for humankind is this realm of the Father, this realm of natural necessity, for our spiritual evolution? The determinism of nature covers all the tasks that freedom brings into evolution. The human being has the global task of working, out of love, on the natural environment, to redeem it, to release it from determinism and bring it into the realm of the law of freedom.

The Son creates another dimension in the cosmos: the reality of the soul as the gateway to the spirit. The Father gives us the body of the cosmos, and the Son gives us inwardness of soul. The soul is potentiality for the spirit, which means the soul is spiritual capacity but not as yet spirit. The soul is capacity for freedom but not as yet freedom. This is why it is so important that between body and spirit there is a soul; for in the soul human beings acquire the capacity for freedom, for the spirit, and in the soul we experience karma as the all-embracing potentiality for freedom. Therefore karma is the source of all the possible ways the soul has of experiencing the spirit. And it is in the human soul that the Son, the Christ, is active, not in order to give us freedom—for freedom cannot be given from outside—but to make us capable of acquiring freedom.

The Holy Spirit is therefore a third and quite different experience. A human being experiences it when he comprehends himself as a being capable of freedom and practises this freedom by realizing it in action.

In other words, we owe to the Father the world of nature as something we can 'liberate', to the Son the world of the soul as inner capacity for freedom, and to the Holy Spirit the power each one of us can create freely in ourselves when we bring to realization this double liberation, the liberation within us and the liberation of nature outside us.

Let us now look in broad outline at the most important laws of repeated earth lives according to which the life of a human being is the effect of his previous life and produces an effect on his next. These concepts come from the spiritual science of Rudolf Steiner, and they obviously sound quite different to someone who has been involved with such things for years or even decades than they do to someone hearing of them for the first time. It is important that the latter do not accept them as dogmas. The best thing is just to listen to them with the intention of finding out what spiritual science has to say — perhaps with the proviso to think about them afterwards and see whether they help to a better understanding of the cosmos and the world we live in. The following descriptions come first and foremost from the lecture Rudolf Steiner gave in Dornach on 24 February, 1924.[3]

Steiner speaks of three possible basic impulses for human action. These three primal impulses are *love*, *hate* and *duty*. Rudolf Steiner describes their effects over three successive incarnations.

One question is: What will be the result in the following incarnation of a life based on *love*? Then we want to investigate how matters develop further if we look at a life of which the fundamental impulse was *hate*. And finally we want to take as our point of departure a life in which the basic behaviour lies between love and hate, meaning a life characterized by indifference. Instead of indifference we could also say *duty*.* So in the third one we start with a life

---

* **Translator's Note**. It is clear to see in what way the author means this; we all know only too well the experience of having to do out of duty something we have no feeling for. The German notion of *Pflicht* is not exactly the same as the English 'duty'. What is meant here are all those motivations which stem neither from love nor from repulsion, but are somewhat *in between*. If one loves one's duty or performs it with enthusiasm, the driving force is not self-overcoming, but *love*!

in which actions are predominantly motivated by a feeling for duty.

Love, hate and duty—these are the three possible basic impulses of human life and action, and no others exist. Any other ones are variations of these three. We could slightly oversimplify and say that everything we do in life boils down to deeds done either out of sympathy or antipathy or an in-between thing, namely, indifference.

If we have a life behind us—let us call it 'life no.1'—in which one of these basic impulses predominated, what can we expect in the next life, in 'life no. 2'?

Let us look at the three possibilities a little closer. What does it mean in our life on earth to do deeds arising out of *love*? Endless things could be said about this, of course. Let us restrict ourselves to a few important aspects. A life filled with love means always reaching out to other people, getting involved, and wanting all the people around one, and who are no less important than oneself, to have things go well. In other words, love is the capacity to be well-disposed to everyone, to help everybody and wish them well. And this power, both of the heart and also of the head, is of the greatest importance. It is the only alternative to seeking one's own advantage at the expense of others.

It is obvious, however, that each one of us has an infinite amount of feelings of hatred *and* an infinite amount of love in us. It happens every day. On no account do I want to say that in one person's life there are exclusively feelings of love and in another's only feelings of hatred, and that the next life will be just as one-sidedly 'like this' or 'like that'. We want rather to see what happens in the next life or the life after that if the first life had a *greater* amount of love in it, or if feelings of hate predominated. There will of course be a mixture of different feelings in each life. However, we can establish the fact that in the areas in which love predominated in the first life there will be in the second and third life something which is the karmic result of love.

Let us think of a person, Francis of Assissi, for example, who radiated an especially large share of love, a particularly large amount of good will, always wanting only the very best for others, and who could rejoice in other people's good qualities (it is a sign of the greatest love if you can rejoice as much in other people's abilities as in your own). Just think how tremendous the forces were which flowed out from this human being, this individuality, to other people—forces which always had a helpful effect, which strengthened the things in them which were positive and brought them further along life's path.

The karmic result of this giving out of love becomes, in the next life, happiness and joy. Where there is a lifetime of loving, a joyful life will inevitably follow. Not a joyful life in the sense that joy streams out from the person himself because he is full of joy. No! What streams out, in one life, from a loving person, from his centre to others in his environment, radiates in the next life from the environment back to him again. Joy does not come from the centre of the person who gave forth love in his last life, but from the manner in which everyone else relates to him. In other words, everybody in his environment behaves to him in a way that makes him happy. They always have good will towards him, and rejoice when things go well for him.

In this second life the stream of force goes the other way, from outside inwards, from the periphery to the centre, which is the karmic result—the inevitable result—of a life where the forces of love flowing from inside outwards, from the centre to the periphery, were constantly positive and supportive.

How and when are these forces transformed? In the spiritual world in the life between death and a new birth. Rudolf Steiner describes in this connection something which I only briefly touched on as I was speaking about the life between death and a new birth. He describes in great detail that in purgatory, and also in the subsequent stages, each of us meets in the spiritual world those human souls with whom we were karmically connected, irrespective of whether they are still alive on earth or also already in the spiritual world.

The soul of the deceased becomes like a mirror in which the inner life of all those souls karmically connected with him are mirrored. It is during this phase that the karmic forces for the following life are gathered up, according to what streams towards us from the souls with whom we are connected.

And what streams back to the person from the souls he constantly loved? Gratitude, good will, and the wish to create a balance and give back good in return! And just because all the souls karmically connected with him thank him by wishing him well, karmic forces arise leading to a following life of joy and positivity.

After a life determined by *love*, in which love streamed out from within outwards, from the person's centre to the environment, and a second life full of *joy*, where the joy streamed from the environment into the inner centre of the person, he dies again and passes once more through the spiritual worlds until descending again to a third life on earth.

The third fundamental metamorphosis of love is an *open heart*, the ability to understand the world. It is the eros of knowledge, the striving for knowledge which gives this person the ability to understand and grasp the phenomena of the world and people immediately, with a clear and penetrating mind. Here again we meet with a stream moving from within outwards, from the centre to the environment. We realize there actually are people who understand the things of the world faster and more thoroughly than others who have trouble in doing so. This is typical of human beings.

We see that the first life in this series proceeded more from the heart, where morality was in the centre, while in the third life knowledge plays the decisive role. All these metamorphoses have of course to be thoroughly investigated. We can only indicate the most important aspects. Anyone who works up a bit more interest for these matters and follows them up more thoroughly will discover an infinite amount.

Let us now consider the opposite: a life based on *hatred*. Rudolf Steiner says that lots of people find it hard to notice hatred in themselves, or to recognize hatred as the basic impulse of many of their actions. The kind of hatred meant here is not only the kind where one wants to kill somebody. What is meant here by hatred is every kind of antipathy towards and rejection of another. Rudolf Steiner especially recommends in this connection that we analyse all the phenomena of antipathy we have in us, including our desire always to criticise everything and everybody. These phenomena are in fact nothing else than variations of hatred, for these are always attitudes of rejecting other people.

We must nevertheless not overlook the fact that the fundamental gesture of antipathy, which hatred is based on, is one of the factors essential to evolution, for without 'antipathy' as the force for marking divisions and for self-assertion there would be no individualization. We may not therefore succumb to the illusion that evolution would be possible without 'hatred'. Later on evolution will go in the direction of redeeming hatred, overcoming it. But initially each one of us must undoubtedly gather a lot of hatred, egoism too; each one must separate himself from others to the extent that he can become an independent self.

However, it is important to be informed—quite objectively—of the fact that all these experiences of rejection streaming from within, from the centre out into the environment, lead in the next life to pain and *suffering*, which go in the opposite direction, from outside inward.

So if I experience that the people round me cause me pain

and suffering because they are not well disposed to me, and would like most of all to pack me off to the devil and hope the worst will happen to me, I must realize — and it really would be beneficial for me to realize — this comes from the fact that in my last life I sent a lot of antipathy, criticism, hatred and rejection towards these very people. I now experience all this in the form of suffering and pain inflicted on me by others.

It has always been I myself who has laid down the causes for all that happens to me. So long as I have not understood this I am living in illusion.

Is karma therefore on a par with fatalism? The answer is definitely not! It has nothing to do with fatalism when we say that our three emigrants found those conditions in New York which suited the inner life of each of them. How would it be if a person who had spent his whole life giving way to his antipathies by criticising and hating, received nothing but joy from his environment? He would be done for, for he would never be prompted to improve himself.

Therefore if a human being in the first life has not opened his heart to his environment, in the next life the environment will send back to him impulses of pain and rejection, and in the third life we have an *apathetic mind*, which is again a stream from within outwards.

Thus we have the following stages:

1. love — 2. joy — 3. an open heart (understanding for the world)

1. hatred — 2. suffering — 3. obtuseness (a dull mind)

The inevitable question will now arise as to which level each one of us is on at the present moment. The answer is on all of them! Each one of us is in many respects at all six stages all the time. It is extremely important to understand this if we want to deepen our perception by means of this all-important image.

In the lecture already mentioned Steiner tells his lis-
teners: 'If someone brings you joy in one life you can be
certain, my dear friends, that this joy is the result of love
you gave him in a previous life.' '... you can be certain,'
says Steiner, for it is impossible that joy will come to me
from another person, that another person will wish me
well, without my having given him the love of my innermost heart in a previous life.

Between love and hatred we have indifference. This is
experienced when all manner of things are done only out of
a feeling of *duty*.

There are things in everybody's life which neither thrill
nor repel him. One simply does what has to be done, what
is expected of one. Everything that is done on the strength
of tradition, convention or routine comes into this category,
which means neither out of love nor hatred. If I hate another
person I hope things will go badly for him and rejoice when
they do. If I love another person I want things to go well for
him. There is a middle sphere, however, in which I am
indifferent. A great many things happen in this sphere out
of convention, routine and habit.

If, in his life on earth, a person acts chiefly out of a sense
of duty, what will flow back to him in his next life from his
environment? Indifference! For a whole lifetime—
throughout his next life—this human being will have to
experience that he does not mean anything to anybody,
nobody is interested in him, nobody either loves or hates
him. If people would at least hate him, but they do not even
do that!

If other people treat me with indifference this is always a
karmic result of my having treated other people with
indifference in my previous life. Indifference can never
come towards me out of the environment if I have not
previously dispensed indifference from the core of my
being. It follows quite clearly that if we want people to take

an interest in us in our next life we must take an interest in them in this life.

After a life in which other people were unimportant to you, and a further life in which you were unimportant to them, there follows a third life in which you are *without direction*. You do not know what to do with yourself. You start something and cannot get on with it, so you start something else, and cannot make headway with that either. You begin to study one thing after another and break off again; you take up a profession but you soon tire of it, and so it goes on. You lack direction because basically you do not care about anything and so it all seems senseless.

Let us assume for a moment that things really are as Steiner describes having seen them in the spiritual world. Is it not most important that if, for example, I lack direction and do not know what to do with myself that I realize this should be attributed to indifference which has been through two transformations? For in the first place indifference flowed out from me into the environment, then it came from the environment and streamed into me. This indifference, which has flowed from two directions, creates or, you could say, leads to a lack of direction, to a lack of feeling for the right path to take. So the third series is:

1. acting out of duty (convention) — 2. indifference — 3. lack of direction

Looking at it, we realize that we cannot change things all that easily from today to tomorrow. The curve of connected phenomena is an extremely far-flung one, and we realize that nobody is in a position to change the fundamental character of his nature in the course of only one lifetime. We know that. But if a person's fundamental character is fixed in the space of one life, we have to ask ourselves how he became like that, and what will he be like in the future. What changes will he go through?

It is up to each one of us to what extent we want to

interest ourselves in and think about this basic pattern, which has only been briefly sketched here. The consequences of this for daily life are infinite, and once we become conscious of this universal law of karma and reincarnation our life can undergo a radical change.

I would like to conclude by quickly touching on a few further matters related to this. In a few of his lectures Rudolf Steiner speaks of the basic tendency to *jealousy* and *lying*.[4] Jealousy is something that takes root in a person's inner being; it is a form of egoism, that is, 'Luciferic'. Lying is a variation of error, therefore definitely 'Ahrimanic'.* Jealousy is the inability to rejoice in the positive qualities of another person, the inability to welcome what he or she is or has. Fundamentally speaking jealousy is the negation of the other person's individuality. Lying is the negation of what we all have in common. For lying is the negation of objective truth, the only thing that can give us the experience of our common humanity.

These two tendencies, jealousy and lying, are also essential to evolution. If these two tendencies did not exist, we could not have become independent and free. Each one of us has to deal with jealousy every day—this quality which makes us want to belittle the unique and inestimable worth of each single human being—and with deceit, which robs us of universality and takes away from us what is common to us all and connects us with objective truth.

It is interesting to see how these two tendencies first of all alter in the course of a lifetime as old age approaches, and how they behave in a changed form in the course of childhood in the next life.

What does the metamorphosis consist of within the framework of one life? In the first place nobody likes to

---

* Editor's note: For further elucidation of these concepts, see Rudolf Steiner, *The Influences of Lucifer and Ahriman*, Anthroposophic Press, 1993.

admit of himself that he is jealous or deceitful. Each of us tries to hide these characteristics. But how does one conceal *jealousy*? By criticising! As a person cannot bear to say of himself, 'I feel jealous,' he tends to criticise everything he possibly can. *Criticism* is nothing else than concealed jealousy. Criticism is the desire to see always and exclusively the faults in others. I have already mentioned the fact that we all of us have this tendency, and if we did not have it we would lack the impulse to be free.

In old age the basic tendency to be jealous works in the direction of making a person *dependent,* and he cannot be independent any more. An elderly person who is dependent on other people for everything, who is no longer capable of making any decision for himself, and who never knows what to do is someone who in his earlier years was full of jealousy. Insecurity, indecisiveness and moral weakness are the inevitable consequences in old age of a basic tendency to jealousy. In the case of an elderly person with these characteristics we can be sure we have an example of someone who earlier in life suffered agonies when he discovered a good quality in another person, or this other person achieved success. Indeed, things of that sort tormented him and gnawed at his very soul.

Jealousy disguises itself in the early years in the tendency to criticise, in the delight at finding wherever possible the hair in the soup, and in old age it expresses itself in the loss of independence and self-confidence.

In the life that follows, the result is a physically delicate or sickly child. If a person has a frail body from birth it is a sign also of a tendency to jealousy in the previous life. What complicates matters is, of course, the fact that if jealousy always causes physical frailty we are not entitled to say that *all* kinds of physical frailty stem from jealousy.

What can we do to strengthen the delicate body of this child? The usual answer would most likely be: Take him to the doctor! Give him such and such a medicine! Spiritual science, however, says that that kind of thing is of less help than telling oneself: This child's body will become all the stronger the more one consciously decides to forgive the child the jealousy which gnawed at it for a whole lifetime. The forces of *forgiveness* will strengthen this child's physical body. This is an example to show that spiritual science actually has quite particularized things to tell mankind, things which reach right down into practical life.

The other basic tendency we mentioned is *deceit* and *mendacity*, the inclination to tell an untruth. All the untruthfulness spoken in diplomatic circles also belongs here. A lot of untrue things are, of course, also said purely for the sake of convention or politeness. We are long accustomed to colouring the truth in thousands of ways. We hide a lot and we distort a lot—just to remind you of newspapers and television. But nobody cares to admit to being a false or deceitful person. I did not tell a lie! we say indignantly. Or we speak of 'white lies', trying to white-wash them.

Steiner calls very strongly on the conscience of present-day people. It is a fundamental psychological law that a person tries to hush up his deceitfulness; and what objective karmic knowledge recognizes as the result of this is *thoughtlessness*, the tendency to take things lightly instead of seriously. Oh well, it is not all that important ... it will turn out all right ... don't worry! This is nothing else than repressed falseness, for if it were not the person would know that truth has to be taken seriously, that one cannot take truth lightly. He would know there is real moral responsibility to be taken where truth is concerned.

The consequence for old age is the basic phenomenon of *evading the issue*. Imagine an elderly person who cannot look another person in the eye. To be afraid of facing a person frankly is always a sign that the relation to truth is disturbed, that this relation is morally doubtful.

And what do we have in childhood in the following life?

A spiritual weakness, a *feeble-minded child*. We shall have a child who lacks the ability to relate to the world.

And what do we do with a child who has told us lies all his life? Steiner says it is essential to tell the child the *truth*, always. And what is the greatest truth? The truth about the spiritual worlds. And where is the truth about the spiritual worlds to be found in its purest form? In fairy-tales! We shall cure this child and make it capable of relating to the world if we tell him the profoundly real truths contained in genuine fairy-tales! This presupposes, of course, that his parents and teachers believe in the fairy-tales themselves!

Lecture Five

SOCIAL RELATIONSHIPS AND REINCARNATION

What effect would it have on social relationships and daily life if human beings were to be aware of reincarnation?

I shall endeavour to show how the social relationships in daily life, the way people relate to one another every day, goes through a radical change if the people who comprise society are convinced there is reincarnation.

I believe that one of the problems which needs to be solved lies in the fact that reincarnation plays only a subsidiary role so long as it is no more than a theoretical conviction. If someone is theoretically convinced of reincarnation but draws no practical conclusions from it, nothing much will change of course! Because the conviction has so to speak not been put into action. If, however, the perspective of reincarnation leads me to alter the way I meet, perceive and think about other people, then reincarnation really becomes a reality that changes life. It takes time, of course, a great deal of time in fact, for it means that a genuine process of change has to be set in train — a process that concerns daily life and takes years.

It is obvious, of course, that knowledge is first acquired as a theory. For when I have understood something I have, initially, merely understood it. Time has to pass until my knowledge affects my daily life, that is, between the understanding of it and putting it into action. On the other hand, though, it would not be honest simply to say that the *theoretical* conviction of reincarnation was not important.

It is just that we should not stop there! The golden thread we shall follow throughout the following reflections is the question: Is it really true that our social contacts greatly change if we are conscious of reincarnation? Does a conscious awareness of reincarnation actually lead to absolutely practical, down-to-earth results for us? Through this new approach to social life does there possibly arise an absolutely new and practical Christianity?

A second question is connected with this: If my life changes in a real way once I am convinced of reincarnation, is this new way of relating to one another really better, really more human? Do I at all costs want to relate to others in this new way? Is this change really of the kind I can say yes to with my whole heart?

Rudolf Steiner's help in these considerations is not just to present them to us theoretically, but he endeavours to show us the practical consequences and the way our behaviour can change towards other people by knowing about reincarnation.

While thinking about this we must not underestimate the basic attitudes which predominate today in the realm of social life. As already mentioned, we live in a materialistic age and therefore we tend constantly — never mind whether this is good or bad — to attach special importance to institutions, to formalities, to business affairs, and to believe that it is these which determine our inner nature. The opposite conviction, that externalities — all that belongs to the economic and social realm — are determined by what comes from our inner life, is less common and seems somehow outdated.

What answer would we give if we were presented with the theoretical question: Does our way of thinking depend on outer economic conditions, or vice versa? For instance, do the owners and employers have a certain ideology just *because* they are owners and employers, and do the workers have a different one *because* they are workers? Does a person's way of thinking depend on his outer circumstances? Or is it the other way round, and a person's inner being determines and shapes outer circumstances?

People keep returning to this question. In theory two answers are possible, and both answers can be right. Why? Because in practice both are possible. A strong individuality is convinced that it is he who determines things, that he does so by means of his inner values and everything that is in him. With regard to a weak personality the opposite holds good; he is weak just because outer circumstances shape his inner life more than the other way round.

Basically, human thinking can manifest in two ways: firstly in a passive-receptive way, in which case it is outer perceptions, together with everything with which the outer world confronts us, which determine all the mental images and reflections we have; and secondly in an active-outgoing way — and this is something which really exists, even if a lot of people refuse to believe it today — when we start out of freedom to activate our thinking ourselves, and to set the stamp of our mode of thinking on the outer world.

What Karl Marx says applies therefore to people who have a weak personality, and this kind of person exists in great numbers nowadays, as we live in an age of materialism. For what is materialism? It is a condition in which externalities and material substance predominate, and determine everything to such an extent that human beings solely react and experience themselves as ineffectual. Karl Marx is right in this respect. It is not a matter of refuting Karl Marx's theory but of overcoming it by changing reality — *our own inner reality*! For the parts of the Marx theory which are true cannot be made untrue merely by our saying they are untrue. The only way we can make the Marx theory untrue is by changing ourselves.

Turning things around — so that the individuality, which once allowed itself to be determined by the material world and now begins to form material existence from the inside — is a process of inner transformation and not a matter of theoretical argument. And when someone has changed himself to the extent that he can say that his inner being, his thoughts, make their mark on outer existence, then Marx is no longer right. And that is not a theoretical statement any more but a real change. Karl Marx is only in error to the extent that he believes the human individuality can invariably be nothing else by necessity than the effect of material existence.

Therefore in spiritual science it is important to take not so much the theories seriously as the basic attitudes. For what we desire to achieve in order that human beings attain to their full human dignity is that each single person reaches the point where he or she forms and creates their life relationships from within, thus presupposing the creativity of the human spirit and enabling these relationships to become human instead of inhuman!

When we ask ourselves what the basic attitude is that arises out of the perspective of reincarnation and changes the whole way we relate to one another, we arrive at a quite specific result. We are asked to make a mental construction of an 'imaginary person'. Steiner speaks of an 'imaginary thought-man'.[5]

Let me explain. If I take my start from reincarnation as a fact, I realize that everything that has happened to me in the past did not depend on chance but that a person — I myself — planned it all with the intention of having it turn out just the way it did. I can construct such a person hypothetically, in thought.

The result is a most extraordinary character, for in my normal consciousness I have been far from desiring a great many of the things that have happened to me. I may even have heartily cursed my fate! And now I am told to construct a person whose view of life was to want, plan for and long for all those things that happened to me!

Steiner gives the interesting example in this connection of a person who experiences something pretty unusual. He is walking along a road in a contented and unsuspecting mood when suddenly a tile falls from a roof onto his head.

The tile did not actually kill him, but it did change his life. The man had tremendous difficulties accepting this transformation, for it signified a radical change in his whole life.

Then he tries to imagine a person (this person really does exist, it is the true ego, the person's higher ego) who has not merely come to terms with a tile falling on his head. No! For even before he was born he chose this event as one of the most important events in his life; he wanted it and planned for it. He looked out for it, after thinking of all the growth potential that would be his solely from a tile falling on his head. That is, out of all the possible events he chose this particular one as the most suitable to help him forward at this point in his life.

On the momentous day itself, while this 'imaginary thought-person' was walking along, he thinks to himself: 'I hope the tile does not have the idea of falling half a metre in front of me or behind me!' He even climbs the stairs of the house the tile is to fall from, loosens the tile a bit to make quite sure it will fall on his head, races down the stairs again and passes the house the very second the loosened tile is bound to fall. And it comes down – ping! – right on his head! And he realizes with relief: 'That is the moment I have been longing for!'

An extraordinary individual! But there really is a person like this. He is there in spirit, he exists spiritually. And if the person all this has happened to does this exercise, he is well on the way to getting in touch with his higher ego. This exercise enables us to accept our karma calmly and with equanimity. Rudolf Steiner stresses that one should do this exercise only with the events one has actually experienced.

If each one of us succeeded better in mustering composure, equanimity and even gratitude concerning all that happens to us, social relations would change drastically and the way we live our lives together would all of a sudden look totally different! Numerous difficulties in this materialistic age of ours – above all those in the social realm—stem from the fact that we have so little knowledge of karma and reincarnation. This is meant in a very real sense.

Our ignorance makes us intolerant towards the things we ourselves have earnestly desired. And it is our very intolerance which makes us take a negative view of the things that happen to us. Instead of seeing all the growth potential arising out of the tile falling on my head I see only the possibilities that are henceforth denied me.

One of the most important changes resulting for our daily life will be that once we are conscious of our karma we shall always see the doors that open up, and these are always innumerable. There is no moment in our development when we could be standing in front of nothing but closed doors. For such a moment would signify the end of evolution. At every moment there are innumerable doors opening. The problem is that in daily life we tend to see the closed doors. Deep down, however, this is laziness, for it is obviously always easier to see doors closing—it certainly comes easier to underline what I cannot do. If I underline what I can do there is no longer any excuse—for then I have to get up and do it!

With regard to relations with other people, every time I meet another person, equipped as I now shall be with this new consciousness, an important thought will arise, and this thought, this conviction, will alter the whole course of this relationship. It will make me realize that I have contributed in part to what this other person is like now; I am one of the people who has made him into what he now is. For if this person is karmically connected with me—and this is seen in the fact that I meet him and we have something to do with one another—this means that we also had something to do with one another in our previous life and I therefore became involved in making him what he now is. And if I wish he were different—'better'—I am partly responsible that he is not 'different' and 'better'. You will agree that once this simple thought has become inner conviction it can bring to my meetings with other people a great deal of tolerance and love. It starts, however, with the conviction of reincarnation and the resulting workings of karma!

There is something else too which, in our daily dealings with ourselves as well as with others, changes radically, and that is our relation to our body. Just how important is our relation to our body is evident from the fact that we have to carry our body around with us for our whole life.

It is difficult nowadays for people to experience the eternal, spiritual individuality of their fellow human beings because we experience their bodily nature so strongly that we tend to identify both ourselves and our fellows with the body.

In fact the relation of present-day people to their body is doubly tragic. It is tragic both from the scientific and the religious points of view.

Science tends to consider the body as the only reality, and says: The body is everything; it is the body which determines a person's soul and spiritual nature. The brain generates thoughts and thoughts depend on the brain. This is why a modern person, moulded as he is by materialistic science, has such difficulty in envisioning that human beings still exist after death, that is, when they no longer have a body.

However, just as science tends to overvalue the body, religion tends to undervalue it. Religion regards the body as unimportant if not actually a hindrance, therefore *one* incarnation is ample; we should be glad, religion says, that after this one incarnation we can finally live only in the spirit.

Human thinking has become so impoverished nowadays (this too is a necessity of evolution) that we often confuse cause with the necessary condition. The brain is the *conditio sine qua non* for ordinary thinking. Consequently, as we cannot think without the brain the brain must be the cause of thinking! That is absolute rubbish! If I want to knock a nail in the wall a hammer is a necessary requirement, for I cannot knock a nail in the wall without it. Therefore, because I cannot knock a nail in the wall without it the hammer is supposed to be what causes the nail to be knocked in the wall! This is the sort of serious error of thought often made nowadays, even by what is called science.

The clear distinction between necessary requirement and cause consists in the fact that nothing, absolutely nothing, happens if all the essential requirements needed for a particular occurrence to take place are available but the cause is missing.

If I have the wall, the nail, the hammer and the picture I have the essential requirements to hang the picture. The necessary requirements are all there, but if only these are there, nothing will happen. For I myself am the cause. Not I myself with my general human characteristics, but as a human being equipped with will-power. The will as such is also a necessary requirement, for even the fact that I am equipped with a will is not enough to ensure that the picture actually gets hung on the wall.

So what is the actual *cause*? The *resolve*, the *decision*! The will as such is only a faculty. If I have the will to hang the picture but never make the resolve to act on it, I and my faculty of will do nothing about it, and the picture never gets put on the wall!

So the brain is an essential requirement for thinking, but the cause of thinking is the ego! After all, the brain is also there when we are asleep. If the brain really were the cause of thinking we should not be able to stop thinking during sleep. The fact that we stop thinking when we are asleep tells us without any doubt that the brain is nothing more than a *necessary* requirement for thinking (there are other conditions that are not essential).

Materialistic science has this tendency to assume that the body is the cause of everything happening both in the soul and the spirit. And we find the other extreme in religion, which says that the body is inferior from every aspect. The perspective of reincarnation enables us to have a balance between these two extremes. How is this? What relationship do we have to our body when we are convinced of reincarnation? Well, to begin with we stop identifying a person with his body. We know that the body we have in this life is something like a house for us to live in. So if I meet a so-called 'black person' or a 'white person' or a 'mixed-race' person I know right away that it is not the person's individuality which is black, white or mixed, but the person's house. The house the person inhabits in this life has this colour. The perspective of reincarnation stops us identifying a person with his body, for every human being inhabits all kinds of bodies in the course of his evolution. We thus avoid overvaluing the body. That is a very valuable contribution to social relationships. On the other hand, we shall not tend, as happens with religion, to undervalue the significance of the body. Now we can begin really to assess the body properly and love it. In fact we shall love our body so much that we shall make an effort to have one time and again. It is in the body, through repeated incarnations, that we seek out, in freedom, all the necessary requirements for our evolution.

When convictions such as these enter daily life, a person does not need theoretical proofs of reincarnation. Someone who lives with an awareness of reincarnation realizes that he owes it solely to the perspective of reincarnation that he is in the position of avoiding the two extremes: the overvaluing or the undervaluing of the body.

Decisive social consequences will arise from this not only with regard to relations between the different races and peoples but also concerning the relation between one person and another, for instance between man and woman where it is important to avoid extremes in either direction.

Before I come to talk about *tolerance* as a basis in the realm of social encounters I would like to add a further example of how the idea of reincarnation can lead to fundamental changes. I refer to the use of abortion and contraception. These two themes have become more and more important in our society in recent years. The question here is what will change if a woman struggling with the possibility of an abortion is aware of reincarnation?

A woman who does not consider reincarnation but who thinks along the lines of western thought and also has a certain religious orientation believes the human soul will be created at the moment of conception. There are only hazy notions of how the soul arrives in the body. When exactly does the soul enter the body? At what point does the embryo become a living person?

If a pregnant woman has no interest whatsoever in things of the spirit, if it does not occur to her that this is a human being, a spiritual being, coming into the world, but considers only her own emotional life and her economic situation and so on, she can of course more easily decide to close the door. Admittedly, numerous doctors stress again and again that not only do many women suffer far more difficulties with an abortion, afterwards, than they had imagined, but that they themselves, after bringing about an abortion, suffer unexpected inner battles.

What is it that changes when we include reincarnation in our considerations of the theme of abortion? It seems to me that in the case of an 'unwanted' pregnancy it is out of place to tell the expectant mother that she 'ought to' or she 'ought not to', apart from the fact that this usually gets you nowhere anyway.

It would be much more important to ask the following questions. How can new and additional strength be found?

Is there perhaps a source from which the woman can draw the strength she imagines she lacks? Does the kind of strength really exist that would help to make her capable of going through with this pregnancy (not out of fear of hell fire or any other traditional do's and don'ts, or fear of what other people will think, but because positive strength can actually be tapped to enable the expectant mother to go through with the pregnancy *voluntarily*)? Do forces exist that could really strengthen the woman and enable her to *want* to do what essentially can only be done anyway if she is really willing?

What help is it to tell someone to apply the kind of strength they do not possess? It is easy to moralize. But to establish morality is difficult. I do not give the stove a lecture about fulfilling its duty of heating the room. I put fuel in it. Similarly the expectant mother does not require sermons or commands but the *actual strength* to enable her to do the right thing.

If she is convinced of reincarnation, an expectant mother knows she can rely on the forces of an eternal individuality who has chosen her as mother. And she knows that this individuality will supply her with all the incarnatory forces at its disposal. Many women who struggle inwardly with the question of abortion would be amazed to find that what they thought they could not do they can not only do very well but actually want to do with their whole heart, once they know that these forces really exist, and they are prepared to receive them. For this individuality wanting to be born either exists or it doesn't. If it really exists, if it is real, then the strength it brings is also real. It is no theory.

It is a fundamental law of reincarnation, Rudolf Steiner tells us, that relationships of choice and blood relationships alternate from one life to another. This means that our karma in regard to the people with whom we are blood-related in one life is normally so strong (though exceptions can occur) that forces arise to bring it about that we shall be connected with the same people in our next life out of a free decision. For what is the fundamental character of relationships based on blood? They are not free! I cannot all of a sudden take another woman to be my mother or another man to be my father; none of us can do that. If you have had someone as a blood relative for a whole lifetime, forces arise which aim at compensating for the one-sidedness of this element of necessity and inescapability. After death the wish arises in us to balance our whole karmic relationships with the people who were our blood relatives by looking for a karmic connection in the next life that will be based on free resolve, and this free resolve will not be possible at the beginning of life but only later on.

Our blood relationships are given us at the beginning of our earthly life; we come upon them ready-made so to say, without our being free. On the other hand we choose our friends ourselves, roughly in the middle of our lives, as we said — and in this we are free.

This alternation between blood ties and chosen friendships is a wonderful thing. In this, we actually experience the concrete social reality of reincarnation and karma. Just think what happens if the expectant mother who is inwardly struggling and looking for the strength to be able to go through with her pregnancy (for in her deepest heart she longs to have these forces) can say to herself: This individuality, this human being is choosing me for its mother — and the relationship between mother and child is the most profound and the closest blood tie there can be — and this is because our relationship in our last life was based on the freedom of choice.

What characterizes a chosen friendship? It arises out of our free resolve. Therefore the expectant mother can say to herself: The relationship existing in an earlier life between me and this incarnating human being was based on free resolve. So it unavoidably contained a maximum of wilfulness. This has resulted in the wish to balance this wilfulness through an unambiguous relationship, a bond comprising objective responsibility. This is why it has chosen me as its mother. If this is so, and this being approached me with this firm intention, I can rely on the forces it brings me. For I too, in my innermost self, will it this way.

The strength of the mother who wants to have the child is only a half of the reserves of strength available in any pregnancy. The other half is founded on the will-power of the unborn child. And when we think of the combination of these two forces, the incarnated human being has actually no reason at all for saying she cannot pull it off. For if the necessary forces were really and truly lacking the pregnancy would not occur.

A pregnant woman can always trust in the fact that the human being wishing to incarnate has chosen *just her* in a most individual and personal way. Even in the extreme case of rape there can be no question of a 'chance' event. Things as important as these do not happen by chance. The mother-to-be may wish to enter into dialogue with her future child, and she will draw added strength from this dialogue. She can be absolutely certain of the fact that her destiny can only confront her with tasks within the reach of her possibilities.

But what if pregnancy is interrupted? A pregnant woman can draw additional inner strength from the objective knowledge that her future relationship to her child will only be made more difficult by an abortion. Both their higher selves are keen on fulfilling the karmic tasks they have envisaged. They will be looking for the next occasion to do this in the next best way. The reason why they had chosen *just this* opportunity was that both of them had thought it to be the most appropriate one for their further development.

On the other hand, a woman having practised abortion before can win positive vigour from this kind of awareness. From now on she will know for sure that the will to continue the karmic relationship remains unbroken and that the future will offer another opportunity for its continuation. The future of this relation can be prepared by a loving conversation with the individuality for whom the door was closed this time, and who is most willing to forgive.

I am now going to speak about what I would like to call the true basis of *tolerance*. My starting-point is the assumption that all the evils in the social sphere can ultimately be attributed to the fact that we are too intolerant with one another. We talk a lot about love, about giving and sacrificing, but if we observe reality we realize we have not taken so much as the very first step in the direction of true tolerance.

Tolerance arises when we have understood and acquired as our inner conviction that firstly each one of us has more than one life at our disposal and, secondly, each of us has to spend our present life in a one-sided way (which cannot be otherwise, seeing that we are in the middle of a long evolution), and thirdly we are given the grace to free ourselves again and again from the extremes we are caught up in (which is why we have the opportunity to incarnate so often); for our successive lives are intended to provide for our balancing one set of one-sidednesses with other ones. That is the course of human evolution.

For the sake of comparison, let us imagine a swing. The movement of the swing in one direction is balanced by the movement in the other direction, and as the swing moves to and fro it enables the person on the swing to experience all the positions through which it passes.

One of the first great extremes in which each one of us finds ourselves is being a man or a woman. Let us assume we live only once. That would mean that none of us could ever really fulfil ourselves as a human being. If we had only one life in which we would be either a man or a woman each one of us could only realize ourselves in half measure, for masculinity and femininity both belong to human wholeness.

We must now be honest with ourselves and ask the question: Am I really satisfied with my one half of being human? Maybe I have become used to thinking so. But have I thought about it properly? Would it not be fairer, would it not suit my humanness better if I were given the opportunity to become a whole person, that is, a human being who can experience both masculine and feminine qualities in him/herself? What kind of loving God would ever have been capable of deciding to grant all of us only half the experience of being human? Why and for what reason?

One of the fundamental laws of reincarnation is that an incarnation as a woman is followed by an incarnation as a man, and vice versa. Admittedly there are numerous exceptions, but this is the fundamental rule. A female incarnation is one-sided and therefore creates throughout life a kind of magnetic force, a kind of overall desire aimed at also experiencing the dimension of human existence not experienced in this life, namely, the male dimension. A male incarnation is just as one-sided. Therefore this also creates the overall urge, the strong desire to experience the other aspect in the next life, in this case the female one.

The people who give thought to this no longer see their own masculinity or femininity, and also the masculinity and feminity of others, in such a one-sided and intolerant way as is often the case. They no longer say, 'Women are like this' or 'Men are like that'. On the contrary, they see in the other gender their own past or their own future — a point of view that will have obvious social consequences. Whoever sees the hidden connections will say to himself 'I was like that myself once' or 'I will be like that myself some day'. In fact once people are conscious of reincarnation the true foundations of social tolerance can be established.

A further important alternation is the one already mentioned between blood relationship and a relationship of choice. I am not free to choose my karmic connection with a person to whom I am related by blood. The fact that I did not have free choice creates throughout my life the wish to meet this person again in a situation where I do have free choice, i.e. to have him or her as a chosen friend, and vice versa. In the spiritual world between death and a new birth this wish is transformed into karmic forces, forces of destiny.

A great deal of intolerance in our dealings with one another comes from wanting to resolve and complete everything in one lifetime. This impatience of ours is the greatest source of intolerance. Because we want to resolve everything in one life we try to force things and to manipulate people, and are anything but tolerant! Social relationships are ruined, and meetings between people are brought into confusion. In one life we cannot put all our relationships right with everybody. In a single life not everything can be 'lived out' to the full. If we try to do this, we are putting great pressure on our relationships, and they become strained to such an extent that this strain eventually becomes unbearable, and our relationships get worse and not better.

A further basic law in the succession of incarnations is that one lifetime in which our own individual development takes central place (that is, everything contributing to one's own progress) is always followed by a lifetime 'for other people', a life spent in the service of one's country, for instance, or for the whole of humanity. This may sound surprising, yet none of us can evade the alternation of extremes. The significance of this one-sidedness is that a person who has a 'natural bent' in the one direction is given the chance of working in the other direction in freedom.

Just think what it could mean, say, for a therapist to know this. If a person is ill or has no sense of direction and goes to a therapist, it is so important that the therapist knows whether this person has resolved to put his own development in the foreground in this life, that is, to use all the possible growth potential to his own advantage, or whether he has decided to devote his life more to others.

If someone has the inclination to exist entirely for others, and also knows of reincarnation, he will not be intolerant. He will not condemn others and tell them they are not in a position to love, they are all arch-egoists and are incapable of helping others. He will say to himself: It is possible that in my next life I shall want to or shall have to be primarily concerned in going my own way; or perhaps I even went my own way, chiefly, in my last life.

Now which is better, to live mainly for oneself or to be there primarily for others? Both are good in a one-sided way! But both at the same time does not work; you have to do one after the other. However, if we do not understand the law of balancing the extremes through reincarnation we shall time and again be intolerant. For anyone who is 'egoistic', which means anyone whose chief inclination is to develop and unfold his own talents, will tell his neighbour: You are wrong, you are intolerant! And his neighbour will reply: You are an arch-egoist!

If we know of reincarnation we learn not to want us all to be the same, for we are not the same. A man is not the same as a woman, and a woman is not the same as a man. Blood ties are not like chosen relationships and chosen friendships are not the same as blood ties. A life in which one's own development is central is different from a life whose main purpose is to contribute to the advancement of a nation or the whole of humankind.

A further type of alternation exists between a life based more on 'faith' and a life spent more in seeking for knowledge. Some people approach the mystery of life by devoting themselves first and foremost to a life of faith, while others want above all to 'understand' it. Both attitudes are justified. If we grasp this, we have created another basis for mutual tolerance.

Just as an awareness of the basic laws of reincarnation and karma can give an entirely new form to daily life and social encounters, this awareness can also give to *Christianity* itself a modern and new form.

The traditional form of Christianity is often considered to blame for its not entering enough into real life, that it is just for Sundays. This objection is frequently justified. Our daily working life has adapted more and more to the laws of the physical world, and here the truths of science and technology apply. Religion has told us of a spiritual world of which our actual human experience has become scantier and scantier. The natural and the moral order of things are drawing further and further apart. The realm of knowledge became the realm of practical life; the realm of faith became more and more a world of the abstract 'beyond'. Materialism and spiritualism both became more and more one-sided. Therefore Christianity as a 'religion' got more and more into disrepute.

In Rudolf Steiner's spiritual science Christianity is made the *basis for life* in a most real and practical way. For either daily life itself becomes Christian or there is no such thing as Christianity. True Christianity cannot exist *alongside* life, it has to be *life* itself. Essential to this living Christianity is an awareness of reincarnation and karma which in itself does not remain only a theoretical dogma but which takes such possession of our hearts that every meeting with another person becomes a Christian sacrament.

I can only experience the eternal, spiritual individuality in the other person — the Christ in him — if I regard his real and essential being to be the result of a long development. Even normal *friendship* consists in not passing over as unimportant and in a superficial way what the present moment shows me of my friend, but in wanting to get to know as much as I can about him and his development. Christian love begins whenever interest awakens for the whole past of a human being and of any living creature. For only when we have this interest, the kind that awakens knowledge, shall we become more and more capable of really mutually *understanding* one another deeply and truly. This deeper understanding, which neither can nor wants to stop at the limits of *one* life, is what true Christian love actually is. For to love someone means, above all, to understand him.

The Christianity of the future is the Christianity of this kind of mutual love among people who want to take into account the many past incarnations spent in the mutual intertwining of destinies, so that a stop can be made to the judging and condemning of one another, and grace can be found to really understand one another. In the Gospels Christ says, making a mark on the ground: 'Judge not, that ye be not judged.' The only ones who have no further need to judge are those who understand others. And the only ones who have real understanding are those who have the will to perceive another person's present characteristics in the light of their past and their future.

In conclusion I should like to point to a few phenomena which are connected with the previous thoughts and which are of importance in everyday social encounters.

Let us take for instance the concept of *loyalty*. This also changes radically if we are aware of reincarnation. If we believe we live only once then what we call loyalty is always bound up with a certain lack of freedom. To demand loyalty in the customary sense is fundamentally nothing else than demanding that every problem in a relationship should be coped with and resolved in one single life. In the end this is nothing but moral blackmail.

If I include the thought of reincarnation in my considerations I understand loyalty quite differently. I take my start from the fact that nobody karmically connected with me can ever opt out of this connection. A karmic connection is a connection of destiny that never ceases. As time passes more and more people join the connection, for by the end of evolution everybody should be linked to everyone else, and we should all form an organic intertwined togetherness in the single body of Christ.

If we reckon with reincarnation then loyalty is founded in the fact that everyone who is connected with me karmically, now, will always be karmically connected with me. It is a matter of finding the right shaping of this relationship each time. And there is time, plenty of time, to sort things out. We do not need to have everything rounded off when one life is over. There is still the chance for unfinished business!

And further, by being conscious of reincarnation our view of *reward* and *punishment* changes radically. When we reckon with reincarnation as a fact, reward and punishment are nothing but illusions put into practice wherever people have lost an awareness of reincarnation. For someone who *is* aware of reincarnation there is neither reward nor punishment. Neither the one nor the other exists for him. For what are reward and punishment?

To reward someone means to want to add something further to what a person has already become; to punish someone means to want to give a person another wallop on the head when his development has run into trouble anyway. The only reward there is is positive growth. The only punishment we can receive is what we have missed out on in our development.

There is nothing to be added to what each one of us makes of himself. It is just as impossible to take anything away. Human nature is, in essence, free, and just because it is free it creates itself as it evolves. It is absolutely impossible to make a person better or worse than he has made himself. Assuming there is freedom and reincarnation, each one of us at each stage of evolution is exactly what we have made of ourselves. Nothing and nobody can alter any part of it.

All the fear instilled into people by those who preach to them about hell fire and all the 'rewards' they are promised in Paradise are no more than moral extortion, which is the polar opposite of freedom. A human being who is the forger of his own destiny and growth needs to be given neither reward nor punishment. When he becomes free, freedom is the greatest reward he can receive; if, however, in the course of his incarnations he should lose the ability to be free, that is the equivalent of hell, and there is no worse 'punishment' than this hell.

Much more could be said, of course. However, I hope that with these few examples I have succeeded in giving you just a little idea of what radical and realistic changes can come about in social relationships if people are conscious of reincarnation, and if our conviction of reincarnation does not remain a mere theory but we succeed in actually seeing it at work and putting it into practice.

To live with the awareness of reincarnation — not only in our heads but also in our hearts — means to become *tolerant*. Once we are tolerant we are already halfway to love. More than halfway, for true tolerance is love.

Lecture Six

REINCARNATION, CHRIST'S RESURRECTION AND THE RESURRECTION OF THE BODY

Today let us look principally at the Christological aspect of reincarnation. This would entail starting with a short summary of some of the basic ideas already presented.

The goal of human evolution consists in man becoming divine, for the Godhead wants human beings to unite with the best that is in them. And the best in humankind is their divine dimension or, let us say, the divine spark in each human being. The concept of the divine is, in spiritual science, identical with the concept of the I, with the concept of the independent, spiritual individuality within human thinking, feeling and willing. Every spiritual individuality who is free in his thinking, feeling and willing is divine.

This is the concept of divinity also presented in the New Testament, as already mentioned. The man born blind is blind because this is the way the independent individuality within him, who is responsible for his own actions, and also divine (i.e. capable of independent thinking and autonomous action), can carry out his intentions externally, which means in the physical body.

This primordial intention to enable human beings in the course of evolution to reach in freedom the rank of god accords with the whole significance of Christ's incarnation. The Christ, the highest divine being of our cosmos, became man to show us that human nature is compatible with divine nature, and that in the course of evolution human nature can be raised, can rise, to the level of divinity. Therefore the Christ Event—in the middle of human evolution—is an anticipation by Christ of all that human

beings can become when they gradually transform themselves into divine beings.

If you think about whether a human being *is* divine or
not, a misunderstanding easily arises. If we take a normal
human being at the present stage of evolution, then in all
honesty we must of course say that the difference between
what has been achieved up till now and the evolutionary
possibilities of humankind demonstrated by Christ is
abysmal. But it is not a matter of a difference in principle.
This difference is not intended to remain as such for ever.
On the contrary this difference is there to be overcome.

However, we can only agree that it is possible to overcome this abysmal disparity between the divine-human
nature of Christ since His incarnation and our present very
human and hardly divine condition if we realize that we
have a number of lives at our disposal. It is quite clear to all
of us that without any shadow of doubt everyone reaches
death nowadays in a state infinitely removed from divine.
For if I assume there is no reincarnation and that we live
only once, then it will always be the case that human nature
and divine nature will remain different in principle. If,
however, I allow that human beings have several lives in
the course of which they have the opportunity to progress
further and further, to make themselves more and more
godlike, quite new perspectives open up.

Over the past few days I have also said that the Christ event
can be given a totally different interpretation if we take our
departure from reincarnation. If we are convinced human
beings live only once, then all that the Godhead pours into
humankind as His divine grace comes as though from
outside, i.e. human beings receive it as something not
belonging to their own nature. Assuming reincarnation to
be a fact, we say that Christ has shown us what a human
being can himself become in the course of his evolution.

Divine grace and divine love actually become much

greater and more profound when the Godhead gives to human beings themselves the possibility of experiencing all the stages of divinity as evolutionary achievements on the basis of freedom. This is not the case if the Godhead bestows the divine dimension from outside, i.e. as something not belonging to humankind.

A God who redeems humankind because they cannot redeem themselves would be the kind of God who would have infinitely less love than a God who gives humankind the ability to rise to divinity in freedom. That is the chief thought running through these days. And if God gives humankind the ability to become, in freedom, more and more 'godlike', then the bestowal of this ability is the greatest gift of grace there can be, for human beings cannot possibly give themselves this ability. And if we say that divine love consists in bestowing on humankind the ability to attain the level of a god in freedom then, to be consistent, I maintain we have to say that in no circumstances is this possible in one lifetime.

I have a sister who is a Catholic nun. She cannot bear it that I am destined for hell because of the 'devil' called Rudolf Steiner. She insists on wanting me to go to heaven. And with the perspectives of her convictions she cannot think and want anything else. She has a lot of love, tremendous love. But I feel (and I think this corresponds to the truth) that her attitude to me is very intolerant, for my sister wants to coerce me to go to her Paradise, and go there at the end of *this* life—for where she is concerned there are no others. That is an objective reality. From her point of view she really only wants the very best for me. It is of no help in daily social life if the other person has the good intention of being tolerant, or that she wants only the best for me. To be tolerant means not only insisting on wanting others to have the very best. To be tolerant also means being able to leave the other person in peace. That is something quite different. Tolerance is the inner composure to respect the other person's path, and not to want to force on him or her either what one considers best oneself or one's own good intentions.

A consciousness of reincarnation contains absolutely no reason for hurry, for otherwise I would also feel forced to want my sister at all costs to study Steiner because if she did not do so she would be eternally damned. I would have to want her to start reading Steiner at last, so that she finally gets hold of the 'right' ideas. Thanks to the awareness of reincarnation the idea does not even occur to me to want her to do so. I tell myself: Each human being has reached the point of his or her evolution where they are at present; and there is time enough for everyone. Rudolf Steiner writes in his *Philosophy of Freedom: 'To live* with love for the action and *to let live* in understanding of the other's will is the fundamental maxim of free human beings' (Chapter IX). It is also the fundamental maxim of a *tolerant* person!

What I was endeavouring to say was that it *must* of necessity lead to intolerance if you think you live only once and you are at the same time not totally indifferent. For the alternative has to be that you do not care. The essential need is *inner* tolerance. I would put a large question mark behind the statement that you can easily be tolerant even if you have the perspective of only one life. I would rather say that if you assume you have only one life there are two possibilities. Either you are intolerant or you are indifferent about a lot of things. The idea that 'everything is relative' is also a form of indifference.

Before I present some positive views of spiritual science relating to the mystery of Christ's resurrection and the resurrection of the body, I think it is important to talk about the Catholic position. I will therefore dwell a little on a document of the International Theological Commission which is given a certain official recognition within the Catholic Church. The document bears the title *Current*

Problems of Eschatology and appeared at the end of 1992. The ninth section of this document is about 'The Unrepeatable Nature and the Uniqueness of Human Life: The Problems of Reincarnation'. I shall read you just those points which seem to me to be fundamentally important to our theme.

There are three paragraphs, and at the end of each one there is a bracketed statement. In the first bracket it says 'Denial of Hell', in the second 'Denial of Redemption' and in the third 'Denial of the Resurrection'. Thus in three small paragraphs the theory of reincarnation is presented as though it denies hell, redemption and the resurrection. Then the following conclusion is drawn:

> These four elements comprising the principle of reincarnation [the first element consists solely in speaking about the claim that human beings live more than once] contradict the essential content of Christian revelation. We do not need to refer any further to the fact that the principle of reincarnation is fundamentally different from the principle which characterizes Christianity. Christianity represents a duality and the theory of reincarnation a dualism.

It is claimed here that duality is the opposite of dualism. So duality and dualism are irreconcilable!

> Christianity represents a duality and the principle of reincarnation a dualism in which the body is merely the instrument of the soul. After each life on earth the soul leaves the body in order to slip into a completely different one. From the viewpoint of eschatology the principle of reincarnation rejects the possibility of both eternal damnation and the resurrection of the body.

These claims are outrageous if, for example, you compare them with Rudolf Steiner's understanding of reincarnation. In fact they could not possibly be more outrageous. Also, everything is being thrown into one basket. The 'theory of reincarnation' is referred to without mentioning which theory of reincarnation is meant. Are they speaking about Buddhism or Steiner?

It is important that we look more closely at these three small paragraphs where it is stated that the principle of reincarnation rejects hell, redemption and the resurrection. If one were to say to Steiner that according to his understanding of reincarnation there is no hell, he would probably ask: What do you mean by hell? Eternal damnation?

Where the 'Denial of Redemption' is concerned I hope I have already made it clear this week that Steiner's principle of reincarnation does not reject the redemption – quite the contrary! It was my intention to present Steiner's concept of the redemption so as to make it clear to you that in his interpretation the redemption of man, which is actually a deification, is not only more realistic but much more substantial and real, and is really taken seriously. For a human being's path through a number of earth lives is his actual redemption and consists of his deification, and this is by the work of divine grace *and* human freedom.

I would now like to ask you for your very close attention. I am going to read you the whole of the three small paragraphs I mentioned, for as I said, they are not very long. I am sure that those among you who know a little of Steiner's work will be shocked at these assertions made by the Catholic International Theological Commission, or which, regardless of distinction, are quoted as having been said by one or another promoter of the principle of reincarnation.

Paragraph One:

There is a law of nature according to which evolution constantly advances until perfection is attained. It is the same law which drives the soul to ever new life, and which allows neither a turning back nor a definite stop. A final state of eternal damnation is ruled out *a fortiori*. After the course of a more or less long series of centuries every human being attains the final perfect state of purely spiritual existence (Denial of Hell).

I can recognize nothing of Steiner in these statements. Absolutely nothing. It is totally wrong. Let us look into it: 'There is a law of nature according to which evolution constantly advances until perfection is attained.' This formulation seems to me to be a very general and abstract way of putting it; but we will let it pass. 'It is the same law which drives the soul to ever new life...' Steiner does not speak of the soul but of the human spirit, the I, the individuality and not the soul. Pre-Christian religions could only speak of the soul, the astral body. So long as no I is there one cannot speak of reincarnation. Rudolf Steiner does not speak of metempsychosis or transmigration of the soul— meaning the passing of soul substance from one body to another—but of the reincarnation of the *spirit*, of the spiritual individuality, the human I. Those are two totally different things. In an anthroposophical-Christian sense it is reincarnation we are talking about and not—ever!—about metempsychosis or transmigration of the soul. I repeat: Metempsychosis (psyche, soul) means the passing of soul substance from one body to another, the soul substance passing out of the first body and leaving it to die. Soul substance without a spiritual ego is characteristic of animals. In the Latin language they had the same root stem for the soul (*anima*) as we see in our word for animal. Animals have this kind of soul substance, namely, the group soul. When a lion or a wolf dies the group soul leaves the dead lion or wolf to enter into another lion or wolf, but it is the same soul substance each time.

Thus Steiner is not talking about metempsychosis or migration of the soul, but of the reincarnation of human beings. In the text I have just read to you there is not the slightest reference to this fundamental difference! The soul and the spirit are being confused as though they were the same thing.

'... which allows neither a going back nor a definite stop'. The opposite is true. Steiner says that it is part of the nature of freedom that a human being can also move in the negative direction. For if a human being could not also evolve negatively he would not be free.

I will now make a slight generalization of what I read between the lines of the Catholic version. However, I should like to premise it with the following. If you approach things that have been said with the honest intention of making a comparison and your sole aim is to listen out for 'snags', you will of course find as many as you like. My aim is to make an honest examination of an official Catholic interpretation, to see what it says about reincarnation.

When the people representing reincarnation have their thoughts distorted in this fashion they do of course sound absurd. This is why I am now spending a few minutes on it. If I were not to do so someone could come along and say that the Catholic position, namely, the arguments their people have against reincarnation, have not been considered at all. The thoughts of the other camp have not even been aired. I really do not want to carry on a controversy. These things mean far more to me than that.

The aforesaid text says: '... which allows neither a turning back nor a definite stop'. As I have already mentioned, many Catholics have far greater difficulties than anthroposophists do with the mystery of eternal hell and the problem of a negative evolution in which not even the Christ can intervene, because this touches on the mystery of freedom. For in the spiritual science of Rudolf Steiner we have the courage to say: It is inherent in the nature of freedom that human beings must also have the possibility to slide further and further in a negative direction.

In a single life a person certainly cannot plumb the very depths of negativity and arrive at a negative level that is in a certain sense final. However, if a human being over the course of several earth lives systematically behaves so as to lose his freedom more and more, becoming unaware of his freedom, so that he becomes less and less free, then finally nobody has the right to alter from outside what this person has become.

Quite objectively speaking, there arises through Rudolf Steiner's spiritual science a far greater readiness, a far greater courage, to speak out and say that the consequences of freedom both in the positive and the negative direction are definitely final, whereas there is evidence of a growing uneasiness among Catholics regarding the question of eternal damnation.

Strictly speaking the problem lies in the little word 'eternal'. This word does not exist in anthroposophy for it is a totally abstract concept. This is why, in connection with the loss of freedom, I talked of a negative level which is 'in a certain sense final'. After this, let us say, 'kind of' finality, there will be other cosmic cycles, and the possibility will arise again to start a new evolution.

Anyone familiar with anthroposophy knows that Steiner speaks of seven great planetary incarnations of the earth. First of all there was the Saturn phase, followed by the Sun and then the Moon phase. At present we are experiencing the fourth incarnation of the earth, as Earth. At the end of this incarnation of the earth as Earth there will be a certain separating of good and evil, which means a certain polarization of them—the good in the sense of the realization of freedom and the deification of man, and evil in the sense of a radical loss of freedom.

The Apocalypse speaks in this connection of the 'abyss of the beast'. Why? Because the first subhuman level, where there is no freedom but only natural determinism, is the stage of the animal, of the beast. Thus a human being who in the course of his free evolution loses freedom more and more ends at the stage of the beast, i.e. at the next stage of natural determinism. This is why the Apocalypse speaks of the abyss in the beast, the abyss of the beast. Rudolf Steiner's spiritual science absolutely confirms this serious aspect of freedom.

There will be a further possibility of evolution both for the human beings who have completed their evolution on Earth in a positive way and also for the human beings who have used it negatively. Not until the future sixth incarnation of our earth, called 'Venus', will there be a still more radical division of good and evil among humankind. Finally, on 'Vulcan', the seventh planetary incarnation of the earth, further 'redemption' will no longer be possible as far as this sevenfold evolution is concerned.

Yet the end of these seven stages is still not the end of all evolution. The idea of evolution ending at a certain point is a totally abstract idea. Evolution never comes to a 'halt'. The possibilities the Godhead has of creating worlds are unlimited. However, the people who have lived through their evolution negatively in this cycle which, according to Rudolf Steiner, is the greatest cycle we know of and which consists of seven planetary phases of the earth (Saturn, Sun, Moon, Earth, Jupiter, Venus, Vulcan) will have their last chance of redemption on Venus.

Steiner describes these things in his lecture cycle *The Apocalypse of St John* and in his book *Occult Science, An Outline*,[6] among other places. Therefore it is objectively wrong — at least where Rudolf Steiner is concerned — to say that the principle of reincarnation denies 'hell'. For the concept of hell is identical with the concept of the extreme negative evolution of freedom. The gradual cancelling of the ability for freedom is what hell is. And the possibility for freedom to develop in the negative direction is, according to Steiner, inherent in the nature of freedom itself.

I know many Catholics who find the idea of 'eternal damnation' so intolerable that they want at all costs that, with the help of God's mercy, everyone shall after all get to

Paradise. Anyone who thinks that way, however, is abolishing freedom.

The second paragraph, where it says that redemption is denied, seems to me to be in a way even more disastrous. I quote:

> Human beings attain the ultimate goal through their own merit. The progress the soul makes in each new life depends on its own efforts. All the evil the soul commits is made good by atonement which the spirit has to take upon itself in new and more difficult incarnations (Denial of the Redemption).

The statements made in this short paragraph are, in my opinion, correct, but the concluding inference in brackets is totally wrong. The argument runs as follows. In speaking of the self-redemption of humankind, the representatives of the principle of reincarnation are ruling out redemption through grace.

There is a colossal error of thought here! It makes just as much sense as if one were to maintain that the assistance of parents stops altogether as soon as a child starts contributing to the decision-making. For it is being said here, in so many words, that because human evolution involves freedom grace is excluded. Why should grace be excluded? Why should the fact of my taking a share in the responsibility for my evolution exclude the other fact that an infinite host of beings are at my side? I owe these beings first and foremost my *ability* to be free — which is an infinite and daily grace! — and in second place the daily circumstances necessary for evolution and which I cannot create myself, but without which I cannot exercise my freedom. Grace and freedom go together very well. In fact there is no grace without freedom, and no freedom without grace!

But the argument here is that where there is freedom, where I myself take part in deciding about my evolution, the other aspect is ruled out. That is poor thinking, very poor thinking!

I will read you these statements once more: 'Human beings attain the ultimate goal through their own merit. The progress the soul makes in each new life depends on its own efforts. All the evil the soul commits is made good by atonement which the spirit has to take upon itself in new and more difficult incarnations (The Denial of Redemption).'

No, it does not work out this way at all. Three people, let us call them A, B and C, are working together at a project. When A takes a step he is responsible for it. A can take a free decision on something. Do B and C then have nothing to do? This is the kind of argument we are dealing with. As a human being takes responsibilty for his own evolution the conclusion is drawn that nobody else, not his guardian angel, not the archangels or any other beings have anything more to do! And then they add in brackets: 'Denial of Redemption'. And this is a document of the Catholic 'International Theological Commission'!

I have described 'redemption' this way: 'Redemption is the unceasing activity of spiritual beings to enable us to exercise our freedom every day. Giving human beings the capacity to be free; putting at our disposal all the circumstances necessary for freedom, is what redemption is. It is an immense grace. Tremendous activity on the part of the spiritual Hierarchies lies behind it, and without this activity the exercise of freedom would be impossible.'

The third paragraph, which concludes with 'Denial of the Resurrection' is a bit more complicated. I will read it to you:

The nearer the soul gets to final perfection the less material becomes the body it takes on in the following incarnations.

It is not true that the soul 'takes on' a body! The soul does not take on bodies that are 'less and less material'! The fact

is that the soul spiritualizes the body more and more, that
the material of the body is transformed. Where would souls
otherwise get these 'less and less material' bodies from?

To go on:

> In this sense the soul has the tendency to be eventually
> completely independent of the body.

No. It is the soul itself or rather the spirit which redeems
and transforms the body. The assumption is being made
here that the body is not transformable, that the earth cannot be redeemed and that the soul becomes more and more
spiritual so that it eventually makes itself independent and
leaves the body. And it is just this which is wrong.

And further:

> In taking this path the soul eventually reaches the final
> stage in which it at last lives in a body-free state, inde-
> pendent of matter, for ever. (Denial of the Resurrection).

Steiner says exactly the opposite. I understand Steiner to
say the exact opposite! The point is not that human beings
become 'independent' of matter, which remains the same
for always, but that there is a gradual transformation and
spiritualization of matter itself, this being the 'resurrection
of the body' in the genuine Christian sense.

I will now look at some important aspects of Rudolf
Steiner's Christology in conjunction with reincarnation.

Because the Christ Being out of love for human beings
guides the destiny of humankind and therefore, right at the
beginning of the evolution of the earth and of humankind,
set the goal that human beings should attain the rank of
free, independent beings, He the Christ Being resolved at
the beginning of Earth Evolution to withdraw from the
body of the earth. To leave us our space Christ drew the sun
out of the body of the earth, and the sun left the earth.

The first gesture of Christ's cosmic love for humankind

was his resolve to allow space for an evolution of freedom, of which the first phase would have to be a negative and egoistic one. This is what comes to expression in the parable of the prodigal son, when the father willingly gives the son his inheritance so that his son can become independent. For the father realizes that his son's actual evolution consists in the attainment of independence—that it is this that will be to his good. It is a matter of taking distance, a matter of giving the other the possibility of taking distance and becoming independent.

Through the fact of the Sun Being departing from the earth body it created the necessary space for evolution to begin, and the first phase of the evolution of freedom is an egoistic one. The first step that has to be climbed on the way to freedom is always an egoistic one. First of all it is a matter of negative freedom, an emancipatory freedom, of separating off and retreating.

Before freedom there was symbiosis, oneness with the mother being, with the maternal cosmos, and that was the primal state of Paradise. If independence is to arise, if we want to have individualization, the first evolutionary step has to be one of detachment. This process is what we call 'egoism'.

Egoism is one-sided, there is no doubt. When boys or girls of 14, 15 or 16 years of age begin to rebel against their parents, society, their school, the Church and so on, we call that one-sided behaviour. Even evolution at large cannot immediately proceed harmoniously in every respect. Evolution always consists of polarities.

The first part of evolution, i.e. until the Christ Event, was therefore 'luciferic'. During this period of time there was an egoistic evolution, one aimed at a negative freedom, a 'getting away from'. We had to become more and more self-reliant and independent of one another, and in this sense reject everything coming from others and which determined our existence from outside.

The second phase of freedom is love. But the second phase cannot occur if the first one has not preceded it. In the second phase of freedom, beginning with the turning-point of evolution, the Christ Event, egoism shall be transformed into love and brought into harmony. The love of one's neighbour must be added to the love of oneself (egoism).

'Love your neighbour as yourself.' This statement infers that each one of us loves ourselves. For it is not asked of us to love ourselves. Love of ourselves is taken for granted. Why? Because it is the overall result of past evolution. Nor does it say: Get rid of your self-love. On the contrary, it says: Just as you have learnt to love yourself now also love your neighbour as well. Add to the one love the other love: 'Love your neighbour as yourself.' In the first half of evolution you were led to the point where you learnt to love yourself by pushing others away — for initially there is no other way of attaining independence, no other possible way to become separate and isolated. You should now remain an individuality and keep the love of yourself and in addition, at the same time, achieve communion with others. 'Love your neighbour as yourself.'

What did the Christ Being accomplish? He permitted the first, egoistic phase by withdrawing and making way for Lucifer and the impulse of egoism. For Christ is not Himself responsible for the evolution of egoism. That is the task of, shall we say, lower beings. Egoism is only one dimension of evolution as a whole.

Evolution as a whole is the evolution of love. Christ left one phase of evolution to Lucifer, the one which produced egoism. In the whole mystery of love Christ reserved for Himself the integration of egoism into the all-round harmony of the being of man.

At the middle point of evolution Christ returned to earth to connect Himself anew with the body of the earth and to bring to humankind all the cosmic forces of love needed to set going the second half of evolution, that of love. Now love is being added to egoism. Love of our neighbour is coming to join love of self. And the goal is to find the right harmony, the right balance between love of oneself and love of one's neighbour.

The ultimate and lofty goal of this dynamic is all human beings becoming one, all the individualities becoming one great organism. In the Gospels Christ quotes a statement which is already in the Old Testament. The Hebraic statement can be interpreted or translated in two ways: 'Love thy neighbour as thyself.' In the middle of evolution I and neighbour are two different beings. When evolution has been completed, however, and we have all become one, the Hebraic statement will have this other meaning: 'Love thy neighbour, for he is thou.' Because he is you, because you are of one body, you should love him. Either you love both or you love neither!

By entering into the man Jesus of Nazareth, the Christ deified human nature in an actual and total sense. Through Jesus of Nazareth, through this 'needle's eye' of the bodily structure of a single human being, the Christ entered through death, resurrection and ascension into the entire earth body in order to create the conditions necessary for the deification of man and the humanizing of the whole earth.

Thus we can look at the Christ Event and say that in the Christ Being we see realized all the dimensions of human evolution which have been made real through grace and freedom. In the Christ Being we already see the realization of all those human dimensions which we, as human beings, can attain in the course of the entire second half of evolution because we have now been given the necessary possibilities — until the end of time.

The 'end of time' means the end of Earth Evolution. After that there will be a kind of new beginning.

Holy Scripture speaks of the 'new heaven' and the 'new earth'. What is the 'new earth'? It means an earthly evolution under new conditions. As I have already mentioned, in Rudolf Steiner's spiritual science this new earth, this new beginning of a coming earthly evolution is called 'Jupiter'. Jupiter means the new earth. But the nomenclature is not important. We can just as well speak of the 'new earth'.

Let us now look at the more practical aspect of the matter. What is the global potential, what is the overall human potential arising out of the Christ Event? The basic law underlying Earth Evolution is that its first half is governed by the process of incarnation, where matter becomes denser and denser, and human beings enter more and more deeply into matter. In the second half evolution goes in the opposite direction, with a gradual pulverizing and dissolving, a spiritualizing of humankind and of matter. In other words, in the first half the unfree bodily substrata of nature — the mineral kingdom, plant kingdom and animal kingdom — were evolved as prerequisites for freedom. What are the prerequisites essential to freedom? Everything which is unfree but which can be made free.

The second half of evolution is put at the disposal of humankind to give us the possibility of liberating our being, which has been integrated into all these unfree realms. For as human beings we combine all three realms, the mineral, the plant and the animal, in our bodily nature. Therefore everything of a mineral, plant and animal nature is part of human evolution. It is given us and incorporated into our being in a threefold way, namely, into our physical body (mineral), our etheric body (plant) and our astral body (animal); it is at the disposal of our free ego so that our free ego can express and exercise its freedom and release everything from its cosmic enchantment, which is of a mineral, plant and animal nature both within and outside our being.

The things outside us are only apparently outside. For instance the air which is outside us one moment is inside us the next. The plants are also outside us, yet when we have eaten them they are inside us. The interaction taking place between the human body and the body of the earth is so subtle that when we look into things more closely we cannot in fact say there is anything of a bodily nature outside ourselves.

The whole body of the earth is the extended human body. So there is nothing on this earth which could be outside human beings. The earth has become the body of Christ, Christ has made the earth into His body, for the earth is the body of man's liberation. With His body, the earth, Christ gives us in freedom and love all the possibilities we need for our evolution.

The archetypal picture of this deed occurred in the Christ Event to initiate the second half of evolution; in His death and resurrection the Christ simultaneously showed its fulfilment. For Christ's death and resurrection show us — in the human body of Christ — what may take place for us over the whole further course of evolution.

The body, the physical body, is not that which we see with our physical eyes. The human physical body is in reality a sum total of forces of the greatest variety, namely, magnetic and electrical forces, forces of gravity, chemical, radioactive and other kinds of forces. This physical body, supersensible by nature, i.e. imperceptible to the senses, became visible to our sense of sight through becoming filled with matter. In other words, the Fall of Man consists in the fact that our physical bodies, which were originally composed solely of supersensible streams of force, took up mineral material along the lines of these streaming forces.

It is not the material part which is the physical body. In fact matter is only the 'filling' of the physical body, and is what makes the physical body visible. Imagine you had a magnetic field but no metallic dust to make the magnetic field visible. You would not say regarding this example that the magnetic forces do not exist. They certainly do exist and they are very real. With the help of a little metallic dust you can make them visible. I then see the metallic dust taking on certain forms. The streams of force were there already, of course. They have not just come into existence. It is simply that they have just now become visible. Matter made the physical body visible in exactly the same way.

The resurrection of the body consists of a cosmic analysis.

The synthesis, the great cosmic synthesis, happened between the 'phantom' of the physical body (which is what Rudolf Steiner calls the original physical body existing solely in supersensible form) and cosmic material, the original 'substance' or 'first matter' of Aristotle and Thomas Aquinas. The universe became visible and perceptible to the physical senses by way of this great cosmic synthesis between what is supersensible and what is cosmic filling, cosmic dust. Christ's resurrection initiated the reversal of this evolution, the great analysis.

As the Being of Christ presented the greatest imaginable burden for a human body to bear — for the forces of human evolution had reached the furthest point they would reach in a body weighted down by matter — Christ's body became in the course of three years so brittle that there was actually the risk that it would not carry Him as far as the Cross; it might have failed Him in the Garden of Gethsemane. The spices applied to the corpse did the rest to turn the material of the body, which was already so porous, almost into dust.

When this human body finally lay in the grave an earthquake sufficed to return it completely to cosmic dust.

And the earth as a living being, the mother of us all, 'trembled' and rejoiced in a literal sense at the death of her 'redeemer', and it is not an invention of the Gospels but true to say that she jumped cosmically for joy because the hour of her redemption was coming, the time when she would finally become free again in the wide expanses of the cosmos. This actual 'startled movement' of the earth which we call an earthquake, which was the earth trembling with infinite joy, opened up a crack in the vicinity of the grave. Through this crack the dust of Christ's body entered the body of the earth as a sign of the liberating dissolution that would come about for the whole earth in the second half of evolution. Our Mother Earth was the first to receive on our behalf the communion of the body of Christ.

To redeem the earth means to give it a resurrection body, release it from the weight of matter and make matter into primeval cosmic dust again, so that it can serve once more as the substrata for new creations.

The concept of primeval cosmic dust corresponds to the Greek concept of chaos. It is the concept of primeval matter. It figures in all great mythologies. When a creation out of nothing is spoken of it does not mean that before the creation there was absolutely nothing. We create out of nothing, for example, when we think creatively. And every fructification within a maternal body is also a creation out of nothing. When something is created out of nothing it means that the usual process of cause and effect, the 'creative power' of that which was there before, is destroyed, dissolved. In other words, the fructified ovum consists of a material, a material substrata that no longer has any legitimate possibility of producing anything. It has no constructive forces of its own any more. Its capacity to be the cause of anything has been 'reduced to nil'.

This is the situation then—when the legitimate process of cause and effect, the 'creative power' of matter is at zero—into which a human being about to incarnate introduces, by himself, his own form-forces, his own capacity to make things happen. Because it has to be the exclusive task of the incarnating individuality to form a body according to his own image, any form-force inherent in the material to produce anything has to be annulled. The material of the fructified ovum has to be deprived of any and every physical and chemical force or the possibility of initiating anything. That is the concept of 'nothingness'. It is not an absolute nothingness but nothing as far as the ability of initiating anything is concerned, as far as the 'creative forces' of the material are concerned. For if, on the basis of heredity and so on, this material were in a position to assert by itself its own formative forces we should then not be able to say that the incarnating individuality builds up a body entirely according to its own image, entirely similar to itself.

The creation out of nothing consists then of two acts. The first is the destruction of the ability of the previous substrata to initiate anything. The second is that any and every ability to initiate anything now comes only from the spirit. You might object to this and ask how it happens that a child looks, for example, like its mother. Actually that happens because the two spiritual beings resemble one another in spirit. For they would never resemble one another in the flesh if they did not resemble one another in the spirit. The reason why the child resembles its mother physically is not because its mother participated by way of the creative power inherent in the material of her body in the bodily construction of the child. No. All the initiating power comes exclusively from the incarnating being. However, because this incarnating being is so profoundly connected karmically with the other being, they have so many spiritual characteristics in common that the material in each of them will be similarly structured.

The counterpart to the mystery of the material substrata of the earth, which is awaiting this global redemption of humankind in order to return to the independent condition of cosmic dust, is the resurrection of the 'phantom' of the physical body out of the grave. It is from the grave of Golgotha that the streams of force of the 'phantom' of the physical body arise, redeemed and restored again to their pristine state. For it is these streams of force of the 'phantom' of the physical body which allow each one of us each time we are born to build up a human body according to 'truly human proportions'. The force structure of the

physical body—and this is the greatest secret of the Fall—
had become degenerate, 'distorted' through its interaction
with matter, with the 'filling'. Through the counter-effect,
the heaviness of matter (and this is the Fall!), the danger
arose in the course of the millennia that the streams of force
of the 'phantom' of the physical body would be weakened
and distorted to such an extent that if the Christ had not
come to earth and given us once more the archetypal image
of the physical body according to the proportions of the free
ego we would by now no longer have been capable of
building for ourselves a body that would be an adequate
instrument in which to develop our ego in love and freedom.

At the death of Christ the St John's Gospel mentions the
fulfilment of two tremendous prophecies of the Old Testament:

'A bone of him shall not be broken.'
'They shall look on him whom they pierced.'

Steiner speaks in detail about these two statements in the
St John's Gospel which, at the death of Christ on the Cross,
were quoted from the Old Testament. The bony structure
determines the 'architecture' of a human being, for instance
our upright position, and he says that it was very important
that the bony structure of Christ should not be 'broken'. The
bones of the two evildoers on His left and on His right are
broken—everything of an ahrimanic and a luciferic nature
'distorts' the form-giving streams of force of the physical
body. However, as Holy Scripture, that is, the law of evolution, said that the form-giving forces of the physical body
of the Being of Christ, of the Being of the I, might not be
touched, the soldiers find Christ already dead, and it states:
'They brake not his legs.'

'They shall look on him whom they pierced.'

The work of human beings on the earth, the ploughing of
the fields and so on, our whole modern technology, is like a

'piercing' of the earth's body. Yet it serves the purpose of enabling us to *look upon* Him whom we have pierced. In other words, up till now we have only seen the *physical-material body* of Him whom we are piercing, we have only considered this. And the promise for evolution runs: Human beings will become capable of seeing, in a super-sensible-spiritual manner, the *Godlike being* of the one whose physical body they have pierced.

Human beings dig furrows in His body, for their task is to cleave the entire body of matter. We *have* to reduce the earth to dust. But this 'piercing' of the earth is only the pre-requisite for beholding the Christ in the supersensible (in the etheric), for experiencing the reappearance of Christ in the spirit. We pierce the earth, we release it from this mortal body and return it to cosmic expanses. However, the real goal of this cleaving of the body of the earth is to behold spiritually the one whose body we are piercing. 'Heaven and earth will pass away, but my words will not pass away.'

I shall conclude with some thoughts about what I should like to call the future 'evolution of the rose'. I am taking the rose as a part of the body of the earth and as the repre-sentative of all matter.

What will the actual development of the rose be like in the course of the coming centuries? How is this develop-ment connected with human reincarnation, the redemption of the earth, the 'humanizing' of all of creation and the Christianizing of man himself?

I shall endeavour to summarize some of the aspects that in my opinion are among the most fundamental of Rudolf Steiner's spiritual science, including his *Philosophy of Free-dom*.

The rose became sense-perceptible, physically percep-tible, in the course of its evolution, out of love for human-kind. Why? Because by making itself physically perceptible human beings can think it. In the first lecture I explained that the sacrifice the cosmos made in becoming perceptible, in taking this infinite bewitchment of all the elemental beings upon itself, the exile and 'execration' into what we call matter, this cosmic sacrifice is offered to humankind as a necessary condition for thinking. The sum total of what is perceptible is the sum total of what is thinkable.

For the people who are dead the perceptible rose is not there any more. Our guardian angel cannot perceive this rose; as perceptible rose it does not exist for an angel. The perceptible rose exists only for incarnated human thinking. 'The Word has become flesh' means that the thoughts of the Gods appeared to us as percepts in order for us to think them.

Now let us for a moment progress a few centuries or a few millennia and continue with the thought that the real rose is not the one we perceive with our human eyes and which is there today and gone tomorrow. The true rose is supersensible; the real rose is an etheric reality. This is why Goethe went on the search for the archetypal plant. The one I see is not the real rose. It is the outer manifestation of the rose. I have to add the concept of the rose by means of my thinking. The perception is a challenge to thinking.

Creative thinking, however, is pure love; it is the greatest act of love there is, for when I think the rose I myself become rose in spirit. The thinking grasp of the true being of things is the same as having communion with them. There is no deeper communion than that of intuitive thinking.

The young Steiner says in his writings on Goethe: 'Becoming aware of the idea within reality is the true communion of man.'[7]

The love for humankind consists in this, that some day we shall reach the point in our development at which all human beings — not only a few but *all of us* — will have the being of the rose within us by virtue of our thinking, for that is the aim of the rose, and that is why it has made itself perceptible (for only through thinking is this possible), when all of us human beings will bear within us in our thought power the law of metamorphosis inherent as a spiritual thought form in the rose. To get a thinking grasp of the rose's inherent law of metamorphosis in all its aspects is no mean feat of thought. That is, when the specific law of the rose, as something constant, will have become a dimension of the human spirit in every one of us human beings ourselves, then the rose will at last be permitted no longer to have to become sense-perceptible.

The evolutionary task for which the rose became sense-perceptible will then have been fulfilled. We shall then be able to say: The rose's being has actually been transformed and has become a real part of the spiritual thought body of humankind. It has resurrected in the human spiritual body. And it will be released from this prison of death and received into the love of human thinking in the fulfilment of its infinite love for the development of humankind itself. Then the rose and all other creatures will be released from this prison to the extent that they become humanized and spiritualized in the actual resurrection body of the human spirit. One lifetime is quite insufficient for accomplishing this.

That is the actual future evolution of the rose, the actual evolution of everything sense-perceptible. These are very inadequate words — words with which I can only falteringly intimate the greatest of all mysteries.

That is the evolution which will lead to the actual resurrection of all flesh in humankind and to the resurrection of humankind in the Being of Christ.

NOTES

1 Rudolf Steiner, *The Gospel of St John and its Relation to the Other Gospels*, Anthroposophic Press, New York, 1982.
2 Rudolf Steiner, lecture given on 15 July 1914 in Norrköping. In: *Christ and the Human Soul*, Rudolf Steiner Press, 1984.
3 Rudolf Steiner, lecture given on 24 February 1924. In: *Karmic Relationships – Esoteric Studies*, vol. I, Rudolf Steiner Press, 1981.
4 E.g. in lecture given on 26 November 1910 in Bremen: 'Life Problems', NSL257 (typescript only). Available at Rudolf Steiner House Library, London and Rudolf Steiner Library, New York.
5 Rudolf Steiner, lecture given on 20 February 1912 in Stuttgart. In: *Reincarnation and Karma*, Anthroposophic Press, New York.
6 Rudolf Steiner, *The Apocalypse of St John*, Rudolf Steiner Press, London 1985; *Occult Science, an Outline*, Rudolf Steiner Press, London 1989.
7 Rudolf Steiner, 'Goethe's Way of Knowledge'. In: *Goethean Science*, p.91, Mercury Press, Spring Valley, New York, 1988.

Also available from Temple Lodge
by Pietro Archiati

FROM CHRISTIANITY TO CHRIST

Christianity as the Essence of Humanity
in Rudolf Steiner's Science of the Spirit

'What we traditionally think of as Christianity is only its cultural form, adopted and developed over the last two thousand years. This represents chiefly human *thoughts and dogmas,* human *institutions, churches and beliefs: in other words all that* human beings *have developed as their response to the Christ Event.'*

Rudolf Steiner said of Christianity that it 'started as a religion but is greater than all religions'. Taking this as his basis, Peitro Archiati reaches beyond the earthly traditions and cultural expressions of Christianity to its true spiritual essence. His survey takes us from the history of an 'all-too-human' Christianity to the history of actual 'Christian' Christianity and its future development through a new scientific approach to the spirit.

Archiati's warmth of expression and clarity of thought bring to life ideas and concepts which for so long have been the reserve of dry theology. It soon becomes clear that the theme of Christianity is relevant to us all—as the very 'essence of humanity'!

128 pp; 21.5 × 13.5 cm; paperback; ISBN 0 904693 83 X